RECLAIMING

A HERITAGE

Reflections on the
Heart, Soul & Future
of Churches of Christ

Reclaiming a Heritage

Reflections on the
Heart, Soul & Future
of Churches of Christ

A·C·U
PRESS

RICHARD T. HUGHES

Reclaiming a Heritage:

Reflections on the Heart, Soul
& Future of Churches of Christ

A·C·U
PRESS

ACU Box 29138
Abilene, TX 79699
www.acu.edu/acupress

Cover · Mark Houston
Book Design & Typesetting · William Rankin

This book is composed in ITC New Baskerville with elements from
Type Embellishments One. Body text is New Baskerville 10/12

ISBN 0-89112-020-3

LCCN 2002105011

❧ 2 3 4 5

CONTENTS

i

PREFACE

Since the publication of *Reviving the Ancient Faith: The Story of Churches of Christ in America* in 1996, a number of people have urged me to write a sequel to that volume that would explore not the history of Churches of Christ but the meaning of that tradition. This book is my attempt to comply with that request.

People outside the fellowship of Churches of Christ may find this book of interest, and I hope that will be the case. At the same time, this book is really intended for Churches of Christ and the thousands of Christians who live their lives in the context of that tradition. Accordingly, I speak frankly in this book of "our tradition," "our heritage," "our movement," and "our founders." In this respect, this book is a very personal treatise, reflecting my own assessment of the faith community in which I was raised and which continues to claim my commitment.

I have broken these essays into two sections. The first deals with theological themes like the sovereignty of God, the frailty of humankind, and the meaning of Christian freedom. The second section deals with ethical issues and with questions like, "What does it mean to live our lives in the context of the Kingdom of God?" If section one affirms our freedom from human constraint, section two affirms our obligations as Christians to serve our neighbors in joyous sacrifice and self-giving love. As Luther put it many years ago, "A Christian is a perfectly free lord of all, subject to none. A Christian is a perfectly dutiful servant of all, subject to all." Here we find one of the paradoxes of the Christian gospel, a paradox we associate especially with Luther and his reformation in the sixteenth century. But if we look closely, we will find this paradox expressed as well in the Stone-Campbell tradition of the nineteenth century. In part, this book is an effort to illumine the two sides of this profoundly biblical paradox in the history of the Churches of Christ.

All the essays in this book have either been delivered as lectures or have been previously published. In those instances where these essays have already appeared in print, I am grateful to their publishers for permission to reprint them here. Chapter one, "Strengths of Our Heritage," appeared in the April/May 1997 issue of *Wineskins*. Chapters two and three originated as the Forrest F. Reed Lectures of 1997, sponsored by the Disciples of Christ Historical Society, and have been published by Chalice Press in *Founding Vocation and Future Vision: The Christian Church (Disciples of Christ) and the Churches of Christ* (1999). I am especially grateful to Professors Douglas Foster and Paul Blowers for their critiques of this material, which resulted in several substantive changes in those chapters as they appear here.

Chapters four, five, and six originated as lectures at the Pepperdine University Bible Lectureship for 1997 and have not been previously published. Chapter seven first appeared in *Re-Forming the Center: American Protestantism, 1900 to the Present* (Douglas Jacobsen and William Vance Trollinger Jr., eds.; Eerdmans, 1998). The concluding chapter originated as a presentation at the 1994 *Restoration Quarterly* breakfast, held in connection with the annual meeting of the American Academy of Religion/Society of Biblical Literature, and subsequently appeared in the *Restoration Quarterly* (Third Quarter 1995).

I am grateful to many people who encouraged me to proceed with this book, but especially to Robert M. Randolph, Associate Dean of Students at M. I. T. and for many years a leader of the Brookline Church of Christ in Brookline, Massachusetts. Most of all, I am grateful to my wife, Jan, who for thirty-eight years has dialogued with me on the "meaning of the Churches of Christ in America." She has prompted me in countless ways to rethink these issues time and again. For the spiritual nourishment and the intellectual stimulation she has given me for all these years, as well as for her enduring love, I am grateful beyond what words can express.

Malibu, California
January 2002

INTRODUCTION

o n e

STRENGTHS OF OUR HERITAGE

Some years ago, my family and I visited the William Tyndale exhibit, on loan from the British Library in London to the Huntington Library in San Marino, California. We know Tyndale, of course, as the first Christian scholar to translate the New Testament from Greek into English. The first edition of that New Testament appeared in 1526.

What a thrill it was to see the very first New Testament printed in the English tongue, and then, in another display, the first complete English Bible. As I looked at those exhibits, I recalled how Tyndale and his colleagues paid the ultimate price for their commitment to place the Bible in the hands of the English people: in 1536, the authorities burned Tyndale at the stake.

As I went from exhibit to exhibit, I could not help but contrast Tyndale's commitment to the Bible and the eagerness with which the English people greeted its appearance with the hundreds of thousands of people in our modern world for whom the Bible is nothing more than an ancient, obscure, and irrelevant book. And I was grateful for my heritage in the Churches of Christ.

A People of the Book

I am grateful, first, that we have been a people of the Book. Clearly, there are ways in which one can

read and understand the Bible that are less faithful
to the core biblical message than others, and we in
Churches of Christ have sometimes read the Bible
from skewed and distorted perspectives. Still and
all, our allegiance to the Bible has encouraged us
to focus our lives and our faith on God and on the
redemption He has provided for us through Jesus
the Christ. For that dimension of my heritage, I am
profoundly thankful.

Second, I am grateful that in our best moments,
we in Churches of Christ have not been bound to
inflexible creeds and opinions but, instead, have
remained open to a change in perspective if we
find that change warranted by the biblical text. I
vividly recall my high school days, when I sought
to convert my friends to the Church of Christ. My
mother, a life-long member of the church and a
woman loyal to her heritage, nonetheless advised
me that I should be willing to change, myself, if my
friends could show me evidence in the Bible that I
had not considered. When she offered this advice,
she meant it, and I took it to heart.

Years later, when I undertook a study of the history of our heritage, I found that many, especially
in the early years of our movement, embraced
the same attitude of openness to change that my
mother urged on me. John Rogers is a case in point.
The preacher for the church in Carlisle, Kentucky
for many years in the early nineteenth century,
Rogers charged that "the *fatal error* of all reformers has been that they have too hastily concluded
that they knew the whole truth.... We have no reason
to conclude, we know all the truth," he argued. "We
have nothing to lose in this inquiry after truth. We
have no system to bind us to human opinion."[1]

---

1 John Rogers, "The Church of Christ at Concord, to
  the Elders and Brethren Assembled in Conference at
  Caneridge, Sendeth Christian Salutation," *Christian
  Messenger* 4 (October 1830): 258.

Third, I am grateful that we have embraced a rational approach to the biblical text. This has not always been the case. In the earliest years of our movement, especially among the followers of Barton Stone in Kentucky and Tennessee, Churches of Christ behaved more like Pentecostals than like the churches we know today. Joseph Thomas, for example, visited many of those congregations in 1810-1811 and reported that these "Christians have an exercise ... amongst them called the JIRKS. It sometimes throws them into the fire, into the mud, upon the floor, upon the benches, against the wall of the house, &c."[2] And the dentist-evangelist B. F. Hall recalled that

> the religion of those days consisted principally of *feeling*; and those who shouted the loudest and made the greatest ado, were looked upon as the best Christians.... We would clap and rub our hands, stamp with our feet, slam down and tear up the Bible, speak as loud as possible and scream at the top of our voice, to get up an excitement. I often blistered my hands by clapping and rubbing them together; and my feet were made sore by repeated stamping.[3]

When Alexander Campbell's dominance over the Stone movement commenced in 1823, the extreme emotional aspects of our movement slowly began to disappear.

Granted, in the intervening years, we have grown so committed to a rational faith that we doubtless on many occasions have been guilty of quenching the Spirit. At the same time, in other ways our rational approach to the biblical text has served us well. It has freed us, for example, from extremely subjec-

---

2 Joseph Thomas, *The Life of the Pilgrim Joseph Thomas* (Winchester, VA: J. Foster, 1817), 186.

3 B. F. Hall, "The Autobiography of B. F. Hall," typescript in the Center for Restoration Studies, Abilene Christian University, 53.

tive ways of reading the Bible that allow the text to mean whatever I want it to mean, given my frame of mind at the moment. Instead, it has encouraged us to discover what the Bible means by discovering what the Bible *meant* in its original setting. This approach has not guaranteed that we would discover the core message of the Bible and, to be sure, there have been times when we have majored in minors and missed the Bible's central meaning. But at least it guaranteed us a fighting chance.

Christians Only, Not the Only Christians

Fourth, I am grateful that the heritage of Churches of Christ includes a rejection of the proposition that we are the only Christians and a clear recognition that there are genuine Christians in all the sects and churches of Christendom. Alexander Campbell, Barton Stone, and virtually all the luminaries of the early years of our movement gladly acknowledged this point.

While many have concurred with this proposition over the years, no one put it better than F. D. Srygley, a turn-of-the-century preacher and staff writer for the *Gospel Advocate*. When the editor of the *Firm Foundation* claimed that "the law of Christ is a wall of separation between the church of Christ and all other religious bodies of whatever name or faith," Srygley objected. "In the midst of all the denominations that beset this age and country, it would be absolutely miraculous if some Christians did not get into some of them occasionally," Srygley wrote. "If there are no Christians in any denomination, it is the only place except hell they have all kept out of." Moreover, there were Christians "in saloons, on the race track, at the theater, in the ballroom, around the gambling tables, in the calaboose, behind the jail doors, and in the penitentiary, and on the gallows." Why, then, he asked, should we be surprised "if a few of the meanest specimens of them should occasionally be found temporarily in the most respectable and pious religious denominations of this desperate and God-forsaken country?"[4]

In this marvelous passage, Srygley points to a fundamentally biblical theme that, while often forgotten in the course of our movement, has never been far from our movement's heart and core. This theme is the recognition that all human beings—even Christians—are finite and therefore flawed and susceptible to gross imperfections. Quoting from the Old Testament, the apostle Paul put it best when he wrote in Romans 3:10–12:

> There is no one righteous, not even one; there is no one who understands, no one who seeks God. All have turned away, they have together become worthless; there is no one who does good, not even one.

Those in our movement like Srygley who internalized this biblical teaching were reluctant to claim perfection for Churches of Christ while judging harshly faithful men and women who labored in other corners of the Kingdom. They knew that even in Churches of Christ, "there is no one righteous, not even one." That confession prevented them from making extravagant and exclusive claims regarding their own religious heritage.

Closely related to this, I am grateful that the heritage of Churches of Christ calls for the unity of all Christians. In the early years of our movement, there were few who claimed that the *Church of Christ* that centered in Middle Tennessee was the one true church outside of which there was no salvation. There were many, of course, who claimed that one could not be saved outside the *church of Christ*, by which they meant the universal Kingdom of God. This recognition inspired a genuine search

---

4   F.D. Srygley, "Are Christians in All Denominations?" in *The New Testament Church* (Nashville: Gospel Advocate, 1910), 65ff.

for Christian unity that unfortunately was relatively short-lived among our people. Instead, a growing number from an early date began to confuse the *Church of Christ* with the *church of Christ*. Still, it comforts one to know that many of our people down through the years have worked passionately on behalf of the unity of all Christian people.

A Sectarian Spirit

Fifth, while I am grateful for the unity impulse in our movement, I also am grateful for the sectarian dimensions of our heritage. It is here that I am most likely to be misunderstood. How could I possibly celebrate the ecumenical thrust of Churches of Christ while applauding, at one and the same time, our sectarian agenda? Aren't these two themes polar opposites?

The answer to that question depends on how we define "sectarian." One can certainly be sectarian by claiming that his or her church embodies the fullness of God's salvation and that all other churches are impostors and usurpers. One can think of this version of sectarianism as *the true church versus the denominations.* I have already made it clear that, in my judgment, that kind of sectarianism stands fundamentally opposed to the Gospel message that demands that we take seriously our own frailties and imperfections.

But there is another brand of sectarianism that squares wonderfully well with the Gospel message. We can best understand this version as *the church versus the values of the world.* How many New Testament passages call us to conform our lives to the values of the Kingdom of God, not to the values of our culture? One thinks immediately, for example, of Romans 12:2: "Do not conform any longer to the pattern of this world, but be transformed by the renewing of your mind."

Unfortunately, many in Churches of Christ have allowed the sectarian dimensions of our movement to become misdirected. They have spent their time opposing other churches instead of resisting the principalities and powers of this world. But the abuse of the sectarian ideal does not invalidate that impulse. It is still a biblical theme, waiting to be reclaimed by those in Churches of Christ who seek to conform their lives to the values of the Kingdom of God.

The truth is that many in Churches of Christ, especially during the nineteenth century, embraced the sectarian spirit in its biblical sense. Here one thinks of a long roll call of the saints, running from Barton W. Stone to David Lipscomb to James A. Harding to J. N. Armstrong to R. H. Boll, among many, many others. To a person, these people embraced simplicity instead of ostentation, advocated nonviolent solutions to human conflicts, shunned material wealth, resisted racism, and risked their own well-being for the sake of their neighbor's good.

Finally, I am grateful for two powerful themes, central to our heritage, that have sustained this biblical form of the sectarian spirit. The first of these themes is the restoration vision. I am fully aware that many in Churches of Christ today have lost faith in the restoration vision, believing it to be inherently divisive. There is ample justification for their judgment in this regard, but those who reject the restoration ideal on this ground risk throwing the baby out with the bath water.

The truth is, the restoration ideal has been a powerful stimulus to countercultural thought and action throughout the course of our movement. It focuses our attention on *biblical* faith and allows us to judge the world in which we live by that standard. It sustained Barton Stone when he freed his slaves—long before the abolition sentiment was popular in the American South. It sustained David Lipscomb when he counseled Christians to refuse to fight in wars but to find peaceful methods to resolve human conflict. And by consistently point-ing us to the Prince of Peace and his ethic for our lives, it can help sustain us even though we live in the midst of an unbelieving culture.

It is certainly true that we can misdirect the resto-ration vision and take our stand on biblical minors instead of biblical majors. But our own failures in this regard in no way invalidate the vision itself.

The second important theme in our heritage that has sustained a biblical form of the sectarian spirit is the theme I called in *Reviving the Ancient Faith* the "apocalyptic worldview." I mean by that phrase an out-look whereby we seek to live our lives *as if* the final rule of God were fully present in the here and now. Such a vision calls for radical and countercultural living, since the Kingdom of God inevitably stands in judgment on the kingdoms of this world.

The beauty of the apocalyptic orientation is the way it encourages us to focus the restoration vision on the major themes of the Bible, not on minor notes and obscure details. If the final rule of God were really present in the here and now, for example, would we spend our time quarreling over the number of cups that ought to be used in communion? Would we spend our time sparring with those in other Christian traditions? Or would we dedicate our energies to living out the ethical mandates of the Kingdom of God?

Most people in Churches of Christ today have no idea that an apocalyptic worldview fueled a wide spectrum of Churches of Christ in the nineteenth century. We find this vision especially in the tra-dition that runs from Barton W. Stone to David Lipscomb and, finally, to J. N. Armstrong. After World War I, the apocalyptic worldview slowly declined among Churches of Christ and is now hardly discernible in our communion at all. But it is a priceless dimension of our heritage and one for which I am immensely grateful. It is also a dimen-sion of our heritage that we need to reclaim.

Conclusions

Some years ago, during the upheavals of the 1960s related to both race and war, some wished to sweep the problems that plagued the nation under the rug and speak only of what was right with America. Many of us will recall a bumper sticker popular in those days that counseled our cultural dissidents: "America: Love It Or Leave It." That approach was singularly unhelpful. It does little good to celebrate the goodness of our culture while refusing to rectify the problems that beg to be addressed. At the same time, it does little good to harp on what is wrong with our society and refuse to take responsibility for needed change.

The same holds true for the church. We know the problems that have plagued Churches of Christ. Critics have pointed them out time and again. But there also is no need to pretend they don't exist.

Still, it is helpful to acknowledge the many strengths of our heritage upon which we can build for the future. It is my prayerful hope that members of Churches of Christ can approach our past with loving criticism, that we will strain out the dross but refine the gold, and bring our communion more fully under the cross of Christ and into greater harmony with the will of God as we discern that will in Holy Scripture.

section
one

KINGDOM
THEOLOGY

t w o

CHURCHES OF CHRIST
& THE MEANING OF
CHRISTIAN FREEDOM

Biblical faith is a radical faith and makes radical demands. Yet in generation after generation, Yahweh's people have gone to extraordinary lengths to tame the biblical God and domesticate his expectations. The Bible tells us that we cannot see God and live. Perhaps that is why we flee from his presence so routinely. When God tells us that he is the Alpha and Omega who transcends our poor ability even to imagine his greatness, we insist on making him over in our own image. When God tells us that He alone can save, we want to save ourselves. When God tells us to serve the poor and the dispossessed, we devote ourselves instead to forms of worship and ecclesiastical structures. Routinely, we substitute dogma for righteousness, orthodoxy for holiness, piety for social transformation, and a whole variety of idols for God himself. Biblical faith is a radical faith, but Christians often go to almost any lengths to turn that faith into something conservative, tame, and manageable.

The Subversion of Reforming Movements

Even when reformers help us to see the true nature of God or point us to the radical demands of the

13

gospel, the historic tendency has always been for their followers to domesticate and compromise that vision within a few short years. I want to explore this tendency by focusing our attention on three Reformation movements of the sixteenth century: Lutheran, Reformed, and Anabaptist. Then, with that context clearly in mind, I want to ask about our own heritage in Churches of Christ. Did we compromise and domesticate the founding vision of our movement? And if so, how and why? In the essay that follows, I want to ask: If we care at all about the legacy of those founding years, how might we reclaim the most valuable dimensions of that legacy and appropriate those dimensions in our world today?

The Reformed Tradition

The Yale philosopher Nicholas Wolterstorff reflects in one of his books on the "radical origins" of his own religious heritage. Wolterstorff has lived his entire life in the context of the Reformed tradition of John Calvin. In its earliest years, this tradition sought to implement the radical hope that, somehow, the world might bow the knee to Almighty God and acknowledge Him as ruler and lord. By the grace of God, Christians might then help transform this world into a kingdom of righteousness and justice and peace.

And yet, Wolterstorff recalls that when he grew up in the Reformed tradition, he "saw very little of that world formative impulse so prominent in its origins." Instead, his tradition was now content simply to maintain a theological heritage and to nurture a particular style of piety. "The piety," Wolterstorff recalls, "came through most clearly in the prayers," prayers like, "We thank you, Lord, for the many blessings you have granted us, and we ask you to remember those less fortunate than we are." Those prayers, Wolterstorff now recalls, communicated the thought "that it was God's business to take care of the oppressed and deprived of the world; our role was simply to pray that he not neglect to do so." Wolterstorff notes that when he was younger, if someone had told him that Calvinism in its early years actually stood for a radical transformation of the social and political order, he would have found that description "comically perverse."

Since then, Wolterstorff writes, he has discovered the "radical origins" of his tradition. "Learning of those origins has given me a deepened appreciation of my own identity. [But] it has also produced in me a profound discontent over my tradition's loss of its radicalism. Why has it become so quiescently—sometimes even oppressively—conservative?"[1]

The truth is, the pattern Wolterstorff describes here repeats itself in virtually all reforming traditions. The first generation typically promotes a radical vision, rooted squarely in some extraordinary insight into the character of God or grounded in new and fresh understandings of the biblical text. The profundity and depth of that original vision attract followers who, for various reasons, share that vision and work for its realization. Most often, however, later generations find themselves unable to keep that radical vision alive. As a result, they tame the original vision into a domesticated and manageable ideology, almost entirely shorn of its original power and vibrancy. While the collapse of the original vision may not occur for many years, it sometimes occurs as early as the second or third generation after the original founding.

The Lutheran Tradition

Luther's reform is a notable case in point. As we know, Luther struggled for years with his own sense of guilt. For a host of reasons, the young man Luther

---

1 Nicholas Wolterstorff, *Until Justice and Peace Embrace* (Grand Rapids: Eerdmans, 1983), ix.

could not imagine God in any terms other than judgment and wrath and condemnation. There was no grace, no mercy, no forgiveness. His sense of God's judgment placed on him an enormous burden to achieve perfection and merit God's salvation. And yet, Luther knew his heart and the depth of his own sin. There was no way he could merit God's favor, and no one knew that better than Luther himself. Luther was therefore a terribly troubled man.

But then, while preparing his lectures for a course on the book of Romans, Luther discovered the New Testament understanding of "gospel"—that profoundly biblical doctrine of justification by grace through faith. Slowly it dawned on Luther that he did not have to achieve perfection in order to claim the grace of God. Instead, God extended his grace to Luther simply because God was love, and God had done this in spite of the fact that Luther could never merit this magnificent gift.

This understanding of justification by grace through faith was for Luther no mere "doctrine" that one must believe in order to merit one's salvation. That, of course, would be nothing more than another form of works righteousness. Instead, this doctrine served as a window that opened onto the liberating grace of Almighty God. Put another way, here was a *particular* biblical vision, but one that broke through its own particularity to allow the young man Luther to feel and experience and know the love and the grace of God. Put yet another way, the doctrine was not the critical issue here, but rather the God to whom the doctrine pointed. For this reason, justification by grace through faith became for Luther a dynamic, life-giving, liberating, and soul-transforming vision.

And yet, by the end of the sixteenth century, some of Luther's followers had transformed the notion of justification by grace through faith into nothing more than a doctrine to which one had to give intellectual assent in order to maintain one's status as an orthodox Lutheran. These people came to be known as Lutheran Scholastics. As far as the doctrine of justification by grace through faith was concerned, the issue for them was not so much the God to whom the doctrine pointed, but rather the doctrine itself. They were far less concerned about transformation of life than about maintenance of Lutheran orthodoxy. As one of my professors at the University of Iowa said many years ago, the Scholastic theologians embroidered onto a fine piece of cloth the words, "Justification by Grace Through Faith," then framed the cloth and hung it on the church-house wall and asked the congregation, "Do you believe it? Because if you don't, you're not a good Lutheran."

In many ways, the Scholastics had moved 180 degrees away from Luther's original vision, even though they used the very same language Luther had used some years before. But why? Why did this radical transformation occur? One reason seems obvious. Luther's reforming movement by the end of the sixteenth century had become an institution in its own right. There can be no question that some felt the need to transform Luther's original vision into an orthodox, dogmatic formulation that could clearly mark the boundary separating Lutherans both from Catholics and from other Protestants.

But I suspect there is more to the story than this. Luther's understanding of justification by grace through faith carried with it the requirement that one recognize one's self as sinful, alienated, broken, and estranged both from God and from other human beings. This is precisely why we are justified by grace and not by works. But how difficult it is to confess and embrace our own sinful nature! How much easier it is to invent strategies by which we can justify ourselves! The motivation must have been powerful, then, to transform the radical notion of justification by grace through faith into a simplistic dogma that one must believe in order to achieve one's own salvation. While it might be difficult to confess one's sins, it was far easier to say, "I believe in the proposition that I am justified by grace through faith." That, the Scholastics imagined, was a quick and easy ticket through the pearly gates.

Without question, the Scholastics preserved the form and even the words of the founding vision, but their understanding of justification by grace through faith had little or nothing to do with Luther's original insight. In effect, they transformed God himself into a tame, manageable, and thoroughly domesticated deity who now had to respond in positive ways to their own affirmations of orthodoxy. Put another way, God was now little more than a puppet on a string. And most striking of all, these changes transpired within seventy-five years of the founding generation.

The Anabaptist Tradition

We find the very same dynamics at work in another tradition of the Reformation period: the sixteenth-century Anabaptists. The vision that inspired this movement was so radical that the people who embraced it were known as the "radicals of the Reformation." What did they seek? What was their vision? What was their dream?

The story began in Zurich, Switzerland in 1523. Huldreich Zwingli, the pastor of the newly reformed Protestant church of that city, urged his congregation to ignore the traditions of the church and the medieval theologians, and to focus instead on the biblical text. That, of course, was a risky challenge for Zwingli to make, since anyone who takes the Bible seriously risks being radicalized by the biblical message.

Not surprisingly, some in Zwingli's congregation took his challenge to heart. As they read the New Testament, and especially the gospels, these people discovered the enormous gap between the teachings of Jesus and the world of sixteenth-century Christendom. On the one hand, Jesus made radical demands. He told his followers, or would-be followers, to find power not in their swords but in suffering and the cross, to sell what they had and give to the poor, to leave mother and father and brothers and sisters and follow him exclusively, to find themselves by losing themselves, and to abandon themselves for the sake of the poor and the dispossessed. Yet, the popular church in sixteenth-century Europe knew little or nothing of this kind of witness.

The problem—according to these Anabaptists—was simply the state church. This arrangement meant that every child born into a European family was automatically enrolled in the state church by virtue of his or her baptism that took place just a few days after the child's birth. Some of these children, of course, grew up to be murderers or thieves or adulterers or liars, or just people without any meaningful commitment to the Christian faith. And yet, they were still in the church.

But those who would soon be known as Anabaptists wanted a church composed only of people committed to living out the radical teachings of Jesus. In point of fact, these people sought neither more nor less than a restoration of primitive Christianity. But for them, the touchstone for understanding the ancient Christian faith was not so much the book of Acts as the teachings of Jesus in the Gospels. They hoped to create a community that would triumph not by the sword but by the cross and by the principle of nonresistance, a community that would shun wealth and status, and a community whose members would care for each other in very concrete ways, but especially for the poor and the dispossessed.

In order to create this kind of radical Christian community, these people proposed to Zwingli that the church in Zurich abandon the practice of infant baptism and adopt instead the baptism of adults, but only those adults committed to a radical Christian witness. This vision meant that, alongside the state church, there would exist a separate church, composed only of committed believers.

It is difficult for us to comprehend today what a revolutionary proposal this was. It was revolutionary because it meant a break with the traditional pattern of the state church, a pattern that had dominated all of Europe for almost 1,200 years. For all that time, the state church had been the glue that bound Christian society into one united Christendom. No one could imagine giving up this commitment. And the possibility that people might have the freedom to choose between a state church and a separate church of convicted believers was a thought that boggled the minds of most who gave it any consideration.

And so, when Zwingli received the proposal that the Zurich church adopt the practice of baptism of adults, he wisely referred it to the Zurich town council for a decision. After considerable debate, the council finally ruled: there would be no adult baptisms, and anyone who either baptized another person as an adult, or submitted to baptism as an adult, would be imprisoned. In time, the penalty would become execution.

In spite of that ruling, there were people committed to living their lives as Jesus taught them to live and who refused to be intimated. And so, on January 21, 1525, several of those who met together prayed to God for courage to do what should be done. Then, as the *Hutterite Chronicle* tells us, "George Cajacob arose and asked Conrad [Grebel] to baptize him…. After that was done, the others similarly desired George to baptize them, which he also did upon their request." And then, the *Chronicle* tersely notes, "Therewith began the separation from the world and its evil works."[2]

---

2 *Die Älteste Chronik der Hutterischen Brüder*, 45–7, in Hans J. Hillerbrand, ed., *The Reformation: A Narrative History* (New York: Harper and Row, 1964), 230–1.

Therewith also began the executions of Anabaptists all over Europe. How many died in all, we shall never know. But they died by the thousands—executed by the sword, burned at the stake, drowned, and murdered in a variety of hideous ways.

One hundred and fifty years later, much had changed among these Anabaptists. One noted historian writes that by then, "the creative and intellectual character of Anabaptism had already vanished."[3] In that climate, a young zealot named Jacob Ammann substantially redefined the meaning of Anabaptism. Anabaptists for years had excommunicated those who failed to take seriously the radical standards of the Christian faith, but Ammann argued that all excommunicated persons should be completely shunned. Ammann also argued that anyone guilty of speaking a falsehood should be forthwith cut off from the church. He further claimed that Christians who shared Anabaptist convictions and helped them in time of persecution could not be saved so long as they remained outside the Anabaptist fold. Finally, "Ammann condemned the trimming of the beard and the wearing of gay clothing, and 'anyone desiring to do so,' he said, 'shall be justly punished.'"[4] On these points, Ammann began to divide the Anabaptist congregations. At a meeting in Niklaus Moser's barn, Ammann excommunicated a sizable group of ministers who refused to conform to his demands, then walked out, refusing to shake the hands of those whom he had expelled.[5] With this action, he began the historic tradition we know today as the Amish.

Today, the Amish in the United States have distinguished themselves especially by their com-

---

3 John A. Hostetler, *Amish Society*, rev. ed. (Baltimore: Johns Hopkins University Press, 1963), 27.

4 Ibid., 34.

5 Ibid., 31.

mitment to preserve traditional folkways. It is true that they continue to embrace simplicity and nonresistance. But they have so completely segregated themselves from the larger world that these fundamental gospel virtues have lost their power to speak in meaningful ways beyond their boundaries to the world in which they live. The world knows them best for their quilts, for their resistance to modernization, for their habits of dress, and especially perhaps for their rejection of the automobile in favor of the old-fashioned horse and buggy. The Amish are good and simple people, and admirable in many ways, but their forebears' commitment to the kind of radical Christian witness that reaches beyond the household of faith to serve a world in need has, for the most part, disappeared.

Common Threads

For all their differences, John Calvin, Martin Luther, and that first generation of Anabaptists shared in common one fundamental commitment. Each was driven by a powerful vision of God. In a period when a church grown too fat and powerful had presumptuously pushed God from His throne, Luther, Calvin, and the Anabaptists were each committed in some important way to allow God to be God once again. For this reason, each extracted from the biblical text a theology that opened a window on the power, or the grace, or the goodness, or the love of God. This was precisely what made each of these movements radical and why each was so effective in its own time. None of these movements committed itself to maintain a mere institution, an ideology, or an orthodoxy of some kind. Instead, each was committed to God and sought to translate God's power, rule, goodness, or grace into the common culture of sixteenth-century Europe.

If we were to ask what specific forms those visions took, it is clear that Calvin affirmed God's sovereign rule over all the earth, Luther affirmed the fact that God alone can save, while the Anabaptists embraced a commitment to radical discipleship and in that way, allowed the grace of God to manifest itself in their daily lives.

In the founding generations of those traditions, forms and structures and doctrines seldom became ends in themselves, but served instead to point beyond themselves to the Source who gives forms and structures and doctrines their meaning. That Source, of course, is God. Put another way, while each of these traditions constituted a particular movement with a particular theology and a particular slant on the Christian gospel, each was able to break through its own particularity to allow believers to see and hear and feel the only legitimate focus of Christian faith, namely, God Himself.

And yet, in all three instances, followers in later years subverted their own traditions precisely because they substituted lesser things for the vision of God that had driven the founding generations. The Reformed tradition substituted piety and academic theology. The Lutheran tradition substituted scholastic formulations and orthodoxies. And the Amish embraced outward apparel, untrimmed beards, and a legal approach to the Christian faith that effectively displaced the original commitment to radical discipleship.

These "lesser things" shared one thing in common. Each represented an effort to tame the Living God and put God in a box. And yet, above all other considerations, God is the Free and Living God who breaks out of our boxes, who transcends our efforts to capture His essence, who cannot be contained by our thoughts and theological formulations, no matter how biblical we may think them to be. How can one possibly encompass God in a particular form of piety? In a scholastic form of orthodoxy? In legal regulations or rules about beards and apparel? How can one tame or manage or domesticate the Free and Living God?

The tragedy of the various forms and structures embraced by later Calvinists, Lutherans, and Anabaptists lay in the fact that they possessed little or no ability to break through their own particularity. Instead, forms and structures often became ends in themselves. Too often, they functioned as roadblocks that obscured the glory of God from the longing eyes of believers, not as windows that allowed God's love and grace to flood the hearts and souls of His people.

Churches of Christ

With this background, then, what might we say about Churches of Christ?

First, we must ask, what was the driving genius of our tradition in its early years? Disciples of Christ argue that the heart and soul of this tradition was its ecumenical thrust, its drive toward Christian unity. On the other hand, Churches of Christ have claimed that the fundamental thrust of this movement has been its passion to restore the ancient Christian faith.

THE FREEDOM TO SEARCH FOR TRUTH

There is merit in both those claims. Yet, we must not forget that in addition to restoration and unity, Churches of Christ in the early nineteenth century also committed themselves to the concept of Christian freedom. By virtue of that commitment, they sought to liberate the minds of men and women from static and oppressive systems, from the boxes into which various theological tyrants had sought to place not only God but their followers as well, and from the hard and brittle molds into which little minds had attempted to compress the liberating gospel of Jesus Christ. Put another way, the founders of our movement were committed to a relentless search for truth, and that commitment in many ways helped define the meaning of the tradition.

In my judgment, one of the finest books on the history of Churches of Christ published in the past fifty years is a book that deals not with the history of Churches of Christ *per se*, but with the history of popular religion in the United States in the early nineteenth century, a story that includes the Churches of Christ along with a variety of other popular religious traditions. Authored by Nathan O. Hatch and appearing in 1989, that book is entitled *The Democratization of American Christianity*. Likewise, one of the finest articles dealing with the history of our tradition is also by Hatch. Published in *The Journal of American History* in 1980, that article bears the title "The Christian Movement and the Demand for a Theology of the People."[6] An outsider to Churches of Christ, and previously unfamiliar with the way we view the world, Hatch was simply stunned by the ringing affirmations of freedom that characterized the founding generation. He was incredulous, for example, that some of Barton Stone's early colleagues could write "We are not personally acquainted with the writings of John Calvin, nor are we certain how nearly we agree with his views of divine truth; neither do we care." After rehearsing this and other affirmations of Christian freedom offered by our forebears, Hatch finally exclaimed,

> This was no mere revolt against Calvinism but [a revolt] against theology itself. What was going on that gave [Barton W.] Stone the audacity not only to reject the doctrine of the Trinity... but also to maintain, "I have not spent, perhaps, an hour in ten years in thinking about the Trinity"? What made it

25

Churches of Christ & the Meaning of Christian Freedom

---

6 Nathan O. Hatch, *The Democratization of American Christianity* (New Haven: Yale University Press, 1989), 68–78; and Hatch, "The Christian Movement and the Demand for a Theology of the People," *Journal of American History* 67 (December 1980): 545–57. The Hatch article also appears in Richard Hughes, Nathan O. Hatch, and David Edwin Harrell, Jr., *American Origins of Churches of Christ: Three Essays on Restoration History* (Abilene, TX: ACU Press, 2000), 11–43.

credible for [Elias] Smith, after seriously debating whether he would be a Calvinist or a Universalist, to remove the dilemma altogether by dropping them both? "I was now without a system," he confessed with obvious relief, "and felt ready to search the scriptures." ... Whatever else the Christians demanded, ... they called for a new dispensation of gospel liberty, radically discontinuous with the past.[7]

Hatch is right. Even a cursory review of the early literature produced by the founders of our movement reflects their preoccupation with Christian freedom and the right of every Christian to search for truth. Alexander Campbell, for example, made this characteristic affirmation in 1827:

> I have been so long disciplined in the school of free inquiry, that, if I know my own mind, there is not a man upon the earth whose authority can influence me, any farther than he comes with the authority of evidence, reason, and truth.... I have endeavored to read the scriptures as though no one had read them before me; and I am as much on my guard against reading them to-day, through the medium of my own views yesterday, or a week ago, as I am against being influenced by any foreign name, authority, or system, whatever.[8]

Many in Churches of Christ today may not discern how radical this kind of rhetoric really is. This is why we must listen to those like Nathan Hatch who found this kind of rhetoric almost shocking. When Hatch read this comment from Campbell, he exclaimed, "Protestants had always argued for *sola scriptura*, but this kind of radical individualism set the Bible against the entire history of biblical interpretation."[9]

---

7 Hatch, "The Christian Movement" in *American Origins*, 28.

8 Alexander Campbell, "Reply [to Robert Baylor Semple]," *Christian Baptist* 3 (April 3, 1826): 229.

9 Hatch, "The Christian Movement" in *American Origins*, 32.

And yet, one finds this emphasis not just in Alexander Campbell, but also in Barton Stone. In *The Last Will and Testament of the Springfield Presbytery,* by virtue of which Stone and five of his colleagues proclaimed their freedom in Jesus Christ, one finds these stunning statements.

> We *will,* that our power of making laws for the government of the church, and executing them by delegated authority, forever cease; that the people may have free recourse to the Bible, and adopt *the law of the Spirit of life in Christ Jesus.*

Or again,

> We *will,* that the Synod of Kentucky examine every member, who may be *suspected* of having departed from the Confession of Faith, and suspend every such suspected heretic immediately; in order that the oppressed may go free, and taste the sweets of gospel liberty.[10]

That document was published on June 28, 1804. Twenty-two years later, Stone was still consumed with a passion for Christian freedom. He wrote, for example, in 1826,

> We must be fully persuaded, that all uninspired men are fallible, and therefore liable to err.... Luther, in a coarse manner, said that *every man was born with a Pope in his belly.* By which I suppose he meant, that every man deemed himself infallible.... If the present generation remain under the influence of [this] ... principle, the consequences must be, that the spirit of free enquiry will die—our liberty lie prostrated at the feet of ecclesiastical demagogues....[11]

Likewise, some of Stone's followers contended in 1826 for "certain inalienable rights." And what were

---

10 Barton W. Stone, et al., "The Last Will and Testament of the Springfield Presbytery," in Charles A. Young, ed., *Historical Documents Advocating Christian Union* (Chicago: The Christian Century, 1904), 20–2.

11 Stone, n.t., *Christian Messenger* 1 (November 25, 1826), 2.

those rights? The rights of "free investigation, [and] sober and diligent inquiry after truth."[12]

These are impressive statements, but none was more impressive than the warning offered by John Rogers, the preacher for the Church of Christ in Carlisle, Kentucky, during the earliest years of the nineteenth century. "The *fatal error* of all reformers," Rogers wrote,

> has been that they have too hastily concluded *that they knew the whole truth, and have settled back upon the same principles of proscription, intolerance and persecution, against which they so strongly remonstrated....* Having, then, full in our view, this fatal rock, on which so many reformers have split, may we studiously avoid it. We have no reason to conclude, we know all the truth.... We have nothing to lose in this inquiry after truth. We have no system to bind us to human opinions.[13]

When one grasps the passion with which the founding generation of Churches of Christ defended what they called the "inalienable right" to search for truth, so much else comes into focus. For example, in the early years of his reform, Alexander Campbell ruthlessly attacked the clergy of the various denominations. But he did so, not because he thought they were wrong on various fine points of theology. Instead, he attacked the clergy because their narrow and provincial dogmatism so often prevented their followers from exercising their "inalienable right" to search for truth. As Campbell noted in 1823, "No class or order of men that ever appeared on earth have obtained so much

---

12 J. and J. Gregg, "An Apology for Withdrawing from the Methodist Episcopal Church," *Christian Messenger* 1 (December 25, 1826): 39–40.

13 John Rogers, "The Church of Christ at Concord, to the Elders and Brethren Assembled in Conference at Caneridge, Sendeth Christian Salutation," *Christian Messenger* 4 (October 1830): 258.

influence, or acquired so complete an ascendancy over the human mind, as the clergy."[14]

One might make the very same point about the protest against creeds that characterized Churches of Christ in their early years. The problem with creeds lay in the fact that they codified truth, and in that way, shut off any further need to search for further light on a given topic. Put another way, creeds put God in a box. Precisely for this reason, the founding generation never intended that rejection of creeds should become a major plank in the unwritten creed of later generations of Churches of Christ. That this has happened time and again is the supreme irony of our movement and only demonstrates how far we have come from the ideals of the founding generation. The truth is, the founders' rejection of creeds was nothing more than an affirmation of the right to search for truth.

ON LETTING GOD BE GOD

But how does all of this connect with Luther, Calvin, and the Anabaptists? Did the search for truth that characterized the founders of our tradition have anything in common with the fundamental goals of those three reforming movements? On the one hand, the answer to this question would seem to be negative. In the first place, our founders were not theologians. Instead, they were practical reformers. Accordingly, they seldom worked out theoretical positions regarding themes like the sovereignty of God. In addition, one could even argue that in many ways, our founders were prophets of self-reliance, urging people to read the Bible for themselves and to bring their beliefs and practices into conformity with biblical standards. From this perspective, it is difficult to see how our founders really shared much in common with sixteenth cen-

---

14 Campbell, "The Christian Religion: The Clergy—No. I," *Christian Baptist* 1 (October 6, 1823): 49.

tury figures like Luther and Calvin who focused
their work so completely on the sovereignty of God
and the frailties of humankind.

And yet, there is another way to read the history
of the early years of our movement. Our founders argued that no human being can capture the
truth, possess the truth, codify the truth, preserve
the truth, dispense the truth, or guard the truth.
Instead, each of us must search for truth, and that
search is a search that is never completely finished.
This was a powerful way of confessing that human
beings are finite and frail and limited not only in
their moral attainments but even in their understanding. This was also a powerful way of confessing
that God alone is truth and stands in righteous
judgment on all human pretensions to capture the
truth, as if the truth could be possessed like a car or
a house or a pair of trousers. After all, God is the
God who continually shatters the boxes in which we
seek to contain Him. This is why the founders of our
tradition always insisted that the search for truth is
an inalienable right of every human being and one
that is never brought to completion. In this way, the
founders of our movement, implicitly if not always
explicitly, testified to themes that stood at the heart
of the Protestant Reformation: the sovereignty of
God and the finitude of humankind.

Further, the right to search for truth was a fundamental presupposition of the other two motifs
that were central to our movement: restoration
and unity. In the hands of the founders of our
movement, the restoration vision challenged and
rebuked those who smugly assumed that their
creeds and systems had captured the essence of the
Christian faith. In the early years of our movement,
the restoration vision was a stick of intellectual dyna-
mite that exploded those assumptions and said to
those who made such arrogant claims, "You are a
human being, and you cannot possibly encompass
the mind of Almighty God." The restoration vision

therefore sent everyone back to the biblical text time and time again.

Yet, when divorced from the right to search for truth, the restoration vision could quickly become a mockery and a sham. Some in those early years, for example, thought the restoration vision a requirement that *others* return to the biblical text time and again, but not themselves, since they had long since found the truth, embraced the truth as a possession, and restored the ancient church in all its purity and perfection. Yet, if we judge by the genius of the restoration vision as framed by the founders of our movement, we must conclude that the restoration vision is legitimate only so long as we conceive of the restoration task as process and search. If we imagine we have fully restored the ancient church, or if we think there is no longer any reason to search for truth, we have at that point turned our backs on the very restoration heritage we claim to embrace.

In much the same way, the passion to search for truth was central to the other major commitment of our movement—namely, the commitment to help achieve the tangible union of all Christian people. As envisioned by the founders of our movement, this ecumenical thrust never depended on the ability of human beings to arrive at the truth or to agree on a set of theological propositions. Instead, it first depended on the fact that God is God and that, by His grace alone, Christian people are bound to one another; second, it depended on the ability of human beings to recognize that they are not God and must therefore never behave as though they are.

Thomas Campbell spelled out the first of these principles in the cornerstone of the Christian movement, the *Declaration and Address*, published in 1809. There Thomas wrote that

> All that are enabled *through grace* [italics mine] to make ... a profession [of faith in Jesus Christ], and to manifest the reality of

it in their tempers and conduct, should consider each other as the precious saints of God, should love each other as brethren, children of the same family and Father, temples of the same Spirit, members of the same body, subjects of the same grace, objects of the same Divine love, bought with the same price, and joint-heirs of the same inheritance. Whom God hath thus joined together no man should dare to put asunder.[15]

The critical terms in this statement are these: "subjects of the same grace," "objects of the same Divine love," "bought with the same price," and "joint-heirs of the same inheritance." Why are Christians one? Because God is God, and because He has extended to each of us the very same grace and bought us all with the very same price.

But the ecumenical thrust of our movement was also rooted in the other side of this coin—the conviction that while God is God, all human beings are sinful and finite and frail. It is therefore inevitable that all human beings, including those who belong to Churches of Christ, will make mistakes, misunderstand the word of God, and misappropriate the truth. If that is so, our founders argued, then we must bear with one another's limitations in tolerance and mutual understanding. There can be no more powerful motivation for the unity of all Christian people than this.

Listen, for example, to Barton W. Stone. "I have too much evidence of my liability to err," Stone confessed, "to make my present opinions a test by which to judge the hearts of my fellow Christians." Or again, he wrote, "Be careful not to wound the feelings of the least Christian of any name. View all the children of God as your brethren, whatever name they may bear. What if they have received wrong opinions of truth? This is no reason why you should

---

15 Thomas Campbell, "Declaration and Address," in Young, *Historical Documents*, 112.

despise or reject them. Consider the best method of correcting those errors." It was for this reason that Stone could affirm as late as 1841, "It is common with us that Baptists, Methodists and Presbyterians commune with us, and we with them."[16] Stone made this statement as an aged man, forty years after he broke with the Synod of Kentucky and helped dissolve the Springfield Presbytery in order to take his stand as a simple New Testament Christian. But the stand he took as a simple New Testament Christian never prevented him from embracing a variety of Christian people who simply failed to see the truth from Stone's particular angle of vision. Here we find the meaning of that classic affirmation: "Christians only, but not the only Christians."

Conclusions

If the twin objectives of restoration and unity stood at the heart of Churches of Christ in the early nineteenth century, so did the theme of Christian freedom. And the theme of Christian freedom pointed beyond itself to the frank recognition that God alone is God and that all human beings are fallible. In this recognition, the "reformation of the nineteenth century" as Alexander Campbell liked to call it, stood shoulder to shoulder in very important ways with the great reformation movements of the sixteenth century—those of Luther, Calvin, and the Anabaptists.

The recognition that God alone is God and that all human beings are fallible served our movement in many ways. It served the goal of Christian union since it allowed the founders to join hands with a host of Christian people in a common search for truth. And it served the goal of restoration since it

16   Stone, "Dr. Worcester on the Atonement," *Christian Messenger* 4 (December 1829): 3; "Letter to J.C.," *Christian Messenger* 4 (September 1830): 226; and "Reply to the Above," *Christian Messenger* 11 (June 1841): 340.

implicitly argued that every Christian must return to the biblical text time and time again, constantly rethinking his or her beliefs and opinions in the light of God's holy word. This is precisely what Campbell meant when he wrote in 1827 that he had "endeavored to read the scriptures as though no one had read them before" him, and that he had kept up his "guard against reading them to-day, through the medium of... [his] own views yesterday, or a week ago." And finally, the recognition that God is God and all human beings are fallible graced Churches of Christ with a profound humility and openness that allowed them to break through their own particularity, even while attempting to recover some very concrete particulars of the ancient Christian faith.

But like the Lutherans, the Calvinists, and the Anabaptists of later years, members of Churches of Christ found it difficult to keep their original vision alive. Within a few short years, some had essentially abandoned the search for truth. Instead, they now began to claim they had fully recovered the truth and restored the ancient church. They elevated their rejection of creeds to the status of a creedal statement and attacked those who failed to see the truth from their particular angle of vision. For all practical purposes, these people had turned their backs on the genius of their own tradition: the conviction that God is God and all human beings are fallible.

In the next chapter, I want to explore how and why this transition occurred. But more than that, I want to ask how it might be possible for us to recover the profoundly valuable legacy that allowed Churches of Christ in their early years to affirm the judgment of God, but also his grace; to affirm the restoration of ancient Christianity, but also the unity of all Christians; and to face both the world and God with openness, humility, and a commitment to maintain a constant search for truth.

three

TAMING THE
RESTORATION HERITAGE

As we explained in the previous chapter, one of the dominant themes of Churches of Christ in our early years was our commitment to the conviction that "God is God and all human beings are fallible." This commitment expressed itself in the unrelenting search for truth that characterized the founding generation.

Yet, within a few short years, a large number of people in our tradition had exchanged that search for a preoccupation with lesser things. Some claimed they no longer needed to search for truth since they now possessed the truth in its fullness. Others argued there was no longer a need to restore the ancient church since the ancient church had been completely restored and now existed in the form of congregations of Churches of Christ that dotted the landscape of the nineteenth-century American frontier. What was needed, these people claimed, was a valiant effort to defend the gains of the past.

The striking thing about Churches of Christ was how quickly this transition transpired. In the case of Lutherans, Calvinists, and Anabaptists, this kind of transition took place by the third, fourth, or fifth generation. In the case of Churches of Christ, we find unmistakable signs of this transition in the movement's earliest years.

In this chapter, I want to ask two questions: 1) What evidence do we have that this transition did in fact occur? 2) What can we do now to reverse that transition and reclaim the genius of our own religious heritage?

The Taming of the Restoration Tradition

It is a simple matter to document the fact that a major transition did occur during our movement's earliest years. If we ask where the responsibility for that transition lies, we must conclude that it lies, at least in part, at the feet of Alexander Campbell himself. It is true that Campbell promoted an unrelenting search for truth when he announced, for example, that he tried to read the scriptures "as though no one had read them before" and that he tried every day to hear the biblical message afresh.

At the same time, by making extravagant claims regarding the nature of his own movement, Campbell helped to subvert the genius of his own vision. For example, he argued in 1830 that "no seven years of the last ten centuries" had done more to hasten the millennial age than had "the last seven" years when he had produced his paper, the *Christian Baptist.* Then in 1835, Campbell announced that his movement had actually recovered biblical truth and restored the ancient church. "Various efforts have been made," he announced, "and considerable progress attended them, but since the Grand Apostasy was completed, till the present generation, the gospel of Jesus Christ has not been laid open to mankind in its original plainness, simplicity, and majesty." Or again,

> We flatter ourselves that the principles ... on which the church of Christ—all believers in Jesus as the Messiah—can be united...; on which the gospel and its ordinances can be restored in all their primitive simplicity, excellency, and power...:—I say, the principles by which these things can be done

are now developed, as well as the principles themselves, which together constitute the original Gospel and order of things established by the Apostles.[1]

Little wonder, then, that Campbell's printer published the first edition of his *Christian System* under the title *Christianity Restored*, or that Walter Scott, Campbell's close friend and colleague, published in 1836 a very large volume he entitled *The Gospel Restored*.[2] Scott, in fact, announced in 1827 that in eighteen centuries of Christian history, he had been the first to "restore to the world the manner—the primitive manner—of administering to mankind the gospel of our Lord Jesus Christ!"[3]

The next several years revealed a major ideological shift taking place in the ranks of Churches of Christ. Increasingly, many expressed their concern to define "the true church" in contrast to all the false churches that surrounded them. There is simply no way to overstate the fact that this concern was something new in this tradition. The founding generation expressed no interest whatsoever in restoring the "true Church of Christ." Instead, they sought to unite all Christians on the platform of ancient Christianity. The shift that occurred in the 1830s toward a preoccupation with maintaining the "true Church of Christ," as opposed to uniting all Christians around the ancient faith, represents a virtual ideological chasm between the goals of the founding generation and the goals of those who now committed themselves to recreate and maintain the "true Church of Christ."

---

1 Alexander Campbell, *The Christian System*, 5th ed. (1835; reprint, Cincinnati: Standard Publishing, 1901), xi–xii, 154.

2 Walter Scott, *The Gospel Restored: A Discourse* (Cincinnati: O. H. Donogh, 1836).

3 Walter Scott, "From the Minutes of the Mahoning Association Report," *Christian Examiner* 1 (November 1829): 5–8.

We find one of the most striking illustrations of this latter preoccupation in the work of a Tennessee preacher by the name of John R. Howard. In 1843, Howard published an article in his own publication, the *Bible Advocate*, threatening people with destruction if they refused to abandon their sectarian, human organizations and identify themselves with the one true church. He called upon these people

> to cast away all your unscriptural names, forms and practices; and return back to the true faith—the pure, original Gospel.... The coming of the Lord, in vengeance to destroy his enemies, cannot...be very far off.... And should you not be found among his true people—his genuine disciples—but arrayed in opposition against them, he will "destroy" you "with the *breath* of his *mouth,* and with the *brightness* of his *coming.*"[4]

Five years later, Howard published a sermon that was widely circulated among members of Churches of Christ since it was reprinted in a variety of publications. As far as I can tell, this sermon represents perhaps the very first creedal statement that defined in substantial detail the beliefs and practices of what Howard called the "true Church of Christ." Ironically, item three in this seven-point creed was the affirmation that "the Church now which has no creed but the *Bible*...is, all things else being equal, the true Church of Christ."[5]

Roughly contemporary with Howard, an Ohio preacher named Arthur Crihfield launched a new gospel paper in 1837 that he called, appropriately

---

4   John R. Howard, "A Warning to the Religious Sects and Parties in Christendom," *Bible Advocate* 1 (January 1843): 82.

5   Howard, "The Beginning Corner; or, The Church of Christ Identified," *American Christian Review* 1 (August 1856): 226–35. This sermon was first published under the title, "Identification of the Church of Christ" in Tolbert Fanning's *Christian Magazine* 1 (September 1848): 267ff.

enough, the *Heretic Detector*. Crihfield apparently thought that the task of restoration had little to do with searching for truth but everything to do with exposing heretics. "Any effort to reinstate the Apostles upon their thrones, and the gospel to its honors, is an effort to detect heresy," he claimed, "since by heresy all the mischief to be repaired, has been brought about."[6] In this way, Crihfield typified a growing segment of Churches of Christ who apparently gave little thought to how they might achieve a richer and deeper understanding of gospel truths, but who devoted themselves instead to attacking their detractors and defending what they regarded as the "true Church of Christ."

The Response of the Founders

It is difficult to exaggerate the theological significance of the transition we have just described. It was a shift from a search for truth to the affirmation that truth had now been discovered and must be defended at all costs; it was a shift from the notion of restoration as process to the notion of restoration as accomplished fact. It is little wonder, therefore, that both Alexander Campbell and Barton W. Stone rejected these claims out of hand. Stone, for example, condemned in 1836 members of Churches of Christ who sought to encompass the truth in *unwritten* creeds and then to exclude those who could not agree with that particular standard of orthodoxy.

> Some among ourselves were for some time zealously engaged to do away [with] party creeds, and are yet zealously preaching against them—but instead of a written creed of man's device, they have substituted a nondescript one, and exclude good brethren from their fellowship, because they dare believe differently from their opinions, and

---

6 Arthur Crihfield, "To. T. M. Henley," *Heretic Detector* 1 (15 May 1837): 132.

like other sectarians endeavor to destroy their influence in the world.[7]

Six years earlier, Stone even rebuked some of the followers of Alexander Campbell for their tendency to reduce the boundless truth of God to a single article of belief and a single practice. "Should they make their own peculiar view of immersion a term of fellowship," he wrote,

> it will be impossible for them to repel, successfully, the imputation of being sectarians, and of having an authoritative creed (though not written) of one article at least, which is formed of their own opinion of truth; and this short creed would exclude more Christians from union than any creed with which I am acquainted.[8]

But what about Alexander Campbell? It is undeniably true that Campbell made extravagant claims regarding the movement he led and thereby contributed to the mindset Stone rejected. At the same time, Campbell remained fundamentally unsympathetic with efforts to turn this movement into a quest to defend the "true Church of Christ." As early as 1826, for example, Campbell recognized this tendency in the movement and registered his protest in no uncertain terms.

> This plan of making our own nest, and fluttering over our own brood; of building our own tent, and of confining all goodness and grace to our noble selves and the "elect few" who are like us, is the quintessence of sublimated pharisaism.... To lock ourselves up in the bandbox of our own little circle; to associate with a few units, tens, or hundreds, as the pure church, as the elect, is real Protestant monkery, it is evangelical nunnery.[9]

---

7   Barton W. Stone, "Desultory Remarks," *Christian Messenger* 10 (December 1836): 182.

8   Stone, n.t., *Christian Messenger* 4 (August 1830): 201.

9   Campbell, "To an Independent Baptist," *Christian Baptist* 3 (May 1, 1826): 204.

Twelve years later, Campbell rejected Walter Scott's audacious claim that he (Scott) had been the one who restored the gospel to the earth. "*To restore the gospel* is really a great matter," Campbell observed, "and implies that the persons who are the subjects of such a favor once had it and lost it." These were claims Campbell refused to make. In fact, he expressed his gratitude that he had never "put the title 'Christianity Restored' nor 'Gospel Restored' to any thing I ever wrote."[10]

In 1837, Campbell engaged in a crucial exchange with a woman from Lunenburg, Virginia. The woman wrote to Campbell to register her shock that Campbell "recognize[d] the Protestant parties as Christian" and found Christians "in all Protestant parties." She understood, she said, that the name Christian belonged to none "but those who believe the *gospel*, repent, and are buried by baptism into the death of Christ."

To those accustomed to the notion of the one true church, Campbell's response must have come as quite a shock. If there are no Christians among the Protestant churches, Campbell observed, then there are "no Christians in the world except ourselves"—a notion Campbell found patently ludicrous. As far as Campbell was concerned, the name Christian legitimately belonged to "every one that believes in his heart that Jesus of Nazareth is the Messiah, the Son of God; repents of his sins, and obeys him in all things according to his measure of knowledge of his will." Campbell affirmed that he could not and would not "make any one duty the standard of Christian state or character, not even immersion into the name of the Father, of the Son, and of the Holy Spirit." And then, in the most critical passage of this all-important article, Campbell wrote,

---

10 Campbell, "Events of 1823 and 1827," *Millennial Harbinger*, New Series, 2 (October 1838): 466.

Should I find a Pedobaptist more intelligent
in the Christian Scriptures, more spiritually-
minded and more devoted to the Lord than
a Baptist, or one immersed on a profession
of the ancient faith, I could not hesitate a
moment in giving the preference of my heart
to him that loveth most. Did I act otherwise, I
would be a pure sectarian, a Pharisee among
Christians.... And should I see a sectarian
Baptist or a Pedobaptist more spiritually-
minded, more generally conformed to the
requisitions of the Messiah, than one who
precisely acquiesces with me in the theory
or practice of immersion as I teach, doubtless the former rather than the latter, would
have my cordial approbation and love as a
Christian. So I judge, and so I feel. It is the
image of Christ the Christian looks for and
loves; and this does not consist in being exact
in a few items, but in general devotion to the
whole truth as far as known.

The fundamental assumption on which Campbell
rested this entire argument was his conviction
that because human beings are human and not
God, they are therefore frail and fallible and may
not always see things exactly alike. Accordingly,
Campbell asked his readers,

How many are there who cannot read; and
of those who can read, how many are so
deficient in education; and of those educated, how many are ruled by the authority
of those whom they regard as superiors in
knowledge and piety, that they never can
escape out of the dust and smoke of their
own chimney, where they happened to be
born and educated!

Based on that assumption, Campbell took it for
granted that

many a good man has been mistaken.
Mistakes are to be regarded as culpable
and as declarative of a corrupt heart only
when they proceed from a wilful neglect of
the means of knowing what is commanded.
Ignorance is always a crime when it is voluntary; and innocent when it is involuntary.

Now, unless I could prove that all who neglect the positive institutions of Christ and have substituted for them something else of human authority, do it knowingly, or, if not knowingly, are voluntarily ignorant of what is written, I could not, I dare not say that their mistakes are such as unchristianize all their professions.[11]

What Was At Stake in This Dispute?

What was at stake in this dispute between Campbell and Stone, on the one hand, and some of their contemporaries, on the other? A casual examination of this exchange might lead us to imagine that it reflected nothing more than the old debates over baptism or the boundaries of Christian fellowship that have stood at the center of our movement for almost two full centuries. But the most fundamental issue involved in this dispute centered on the nature of God. Was God free to define the truth, or must God conform to our definitions and understandings? Was God free to accept into the church those whom he chose to accept, or must God bow to our decision regarding who is legitimately Christian and who is not? Was God free to save those He wished to save, or must God save only those whom we have determined are fit for his Kingdom?

To put this another way—when the founders insisted that the Christian walk is a perpetual search for truth, they implicitly affirmed their conviction that God is God, that He is All Truth and All Wisdom, that He is the Transcendent One whose ways are not our ways, and that His thoughts are beyond our thoughts as the heavens are beyond the earth. At the same time, by insisting that the Christian walk is a perpetual search for truth, the

---

11 Campbell, "Any Christians Among Protestant Parties," *Millennial Harbinger*, New Series, 1 (September 1837): 411-3.

founders also affirmed that human beings are finite
and fundamentally flawed, and because we inevitably possess profound and far-reaching limitations,
we simply cannot comprehend the mind of God.
For this reason, we have only one legitimate choice:
we must let God be God.

The founders obviously believed that there is
much we can know about God from the revelation
He has given to us in Jesus Christ and from the
God-inspired witness to that revelation which is the
biblical text. At the same time, they also believed
that there is much we do not know, and much that
we will inevitably misunderstand and misinterpret.
This is precisely why Campbell felt the need to
reevaluate his own presuppositions day after day
after day. In fact, Campbell never thought the day
would come when there would be no need for that
re-evaluation process.

In other words, the founders believed the great
biblical truth that God is God and that human
beings are human beings, and that a great gulf
exists between the two. Their commitment to the
Kingdom of God, on the one hand, and to Christian
freedom, on the other, leads me to conclude that
they took seriously words like these from the
prophet Isaiah:

> Who has understood the mind of the Lord,
> or instructed him as his counselor?
> (Isaiah 40:13)

> Do you not know?
> Have you not heard?
> The Lord is the everlasting God,
> the Creator of the ends of the earth.
> He will not grow tired or weary,
> and his understanding no man can fathom.
> (Isaiah 40:28)

They must have taken very seriously Isaiah's report
that when he saw the Lord, "seated on a throne,
high and exalted," he could only respond with those
self-revealing words, "Woe to me! I am ruined! For I
am a man of unclean lips, and I live among a people

of unclean lips, and my eyes have seen the King, the
Lord Almighty" (Isaiah 6:5).

In addition, they must have taken seriously God's
speech to Job, "Who is this that darkens my coun-
sel with words without knowledge?" (Job 38:2) and
Job's response to God,

> You asked, "Who is this that obscures my
> counsel without knowledge?
> Surely I spoke of things I did not understand,
> things too wonderful for me to know.
>
> You said, "Listen now, and I will speak;
> I will question you,
> and you shall answer me."
> My ears had heard of you
> but now my eyes have seen you.
> Therefore I despise myself
> and repent in dust and ashes. (Job 42:3–6)

Alexander Campbell and Barton W. Stone surely
believed the promise, "You shall know the truth
and the truth shall make you free." (Jn. 8:32) But
based on everything we know about those men, they
understood that the truth that would make us free
was not a static set of propositions about the church
or the plan of salvation or the five acts of worship
or how we should organize our congregations.
Rather, they knew that the truth that would set us
free was the truth that God is God, that all human
beings are finite and frail and fallible, and that we
are therefore saved, not by our knowledge or our
works or our ability finally to restore the ancient
church in its every detail, but simply by virtue of
God's incredible grace, offered to us in his Son,
Jesus the Christ.

On the other hand, when some began to argue
that truth had been recovered and the ancient
church restored, and when they launched their
defense of the one "true Church of Christ" in oppo-
sition to those who saw things from a different angle
of vision, precisely at that point those who made
these claims compromised the most fundamental
presupposition of our movement. In effect, they

transformed the Stone-Campbell movement into a profoundly humanistic movement that trusted not so much in the power of God as in the ability of self-sufficient human beings to get things right and, for all practical purposes, to save themselves.

Perhaps even more important, those who made this change placed the Lord of heaven and earth in a very small box, whose walls they built of human judgment and human interpretation. The builders of this box imagined these walls were firm and secure since, from their limited angle of vision, they seemed altogether rational and fundamentally biblical. But they failed to acknowledge the fact that the Lord of Heaven and Earth shatters every box in which we seek to place him; refuses to be confined by words, even biblical words; and therefore shatters every formula, every definition, every pattern, every plan, and every form of orthodoxy we can possibly devise to contain him. Simply put, the builders of the box sought to manage a God who will not be managed.

How Did We Lose Our Way? How Can We Find Our Way Home?

The irony in this development is unmistakable. How could those who so strongly objected to creeds and human systems have finally put God in a box? That is an interesting question, but a far more pressing question is this: How can we in our generation embrace a more biblical doctrine of God? How can we catch a fuller vision of his greatness and glory and power? And on the other side of the coin, how can we embrace a more realistic assessment of our own limitations and failures? How can we acknowledge the many ways in which our own wisdom and understanding simply fail to serve us as well as we might wish?

For all practical purposes, these questions are all one question and point to the same consistent answer that is simply this: we must embrace the truth that we, too, are human beings. That may seem a strange thing to say since it is so obvious. And yet, for almost two hundred years, we have sought in various ways to deny our humanness and to affirm that we are something we are not. We have done this because we have so often confused the ideals we embrace with the reality of our present situation.

For example, we have aspired for many years to restore the purity of the ancient church of Jesus Christ. That has been an ideal. But in our zeal to implement that ideal, we have sometimes allowed ourselves to believe that we have no human founders whatsoever, no history but the story of the faithful recorded in the biblical text, no theology but the Bible itself, and that, in fact, we ourselves are nothing more and nothing less than the church of the first Christian age. When we make these kinds of assumptions, we implicitly deny the fact that we are real human beings living in real human history.

The question of our own human history is in many ways the fundamental question we must address in this regard. Once, when I was teaching at one of our Christian universities and attending one of the largest congregations of Churches of Christ in that city, I taught a Sunday school class for junior high school students on the history of Christianity. Most of the twenty-five or thirty students in that class were children of professors at that Christian university. We began in the beginning, with the day of Pentecost, then slowly made our way through the history of the church. We explored the early persecutions, the Apostolic Fathers, Augustine, Aquinas, Luther, Calvin, Zwingli, the Anabaptists, and the Puritans. Then, finally, the day came for the exploration of the history of our own particular movement in the United States. I thought surely some of the students would know something already about Alexander Campbell and Barton W.

Stone, at the very least. After all, these children had been raised in the Church of Christ and, more than that, had lived their lives in the context of a Christian university where most of their parents worked. How could they possibly avoid knowing about the heritage of our movement?

And so I began class that morning by asking the simple question, "How many of you know the name Alexander Campbell?" To my surprise, I got only fish eyes. "How many of you know the name Barton W. Stone?" Fish eyes, once again. It turned out that in that class of twenty-five or thirty students, each of them raised in the very bosom of the Churches of Christ, only one child had ever so much as heard the names Alexander Campbell and Barton W. Stone. That child was my own son, Andy.

It occurred to me that day that these students knew nothing about their own religious heritage because many of their mothers and fathers along with many of the members of that congregation finally thought this kind of knowledge fundamentally irrelevant. Because they sought to be New Testament Christians, not Campbellites or Stoneites, and in their zeal to claim authentic biblical faith rather than some nineteenth-century version of that biblical faith, they implicitly denied their own history. No wonder their children had never heard of Alexander Campbell or Barton W. Stone.

And yet, there is no possible way we can escape our history. We are, after all, human beings. We *have* been shaped in countless ways by Alexander Campbell and Barton Stone, by Tolbert Fanning and Moses Lard, by Benjamin Franklin and David Lipscomb, and by so many others whose names we may not know but who nonetheless helped define our very particular tradition. This is why, throughout this chapter and the one before it, I have acknowledged Alexander Campbell and Barton Stone as two of the "founders" of our tradition. To make that confession in no way detracts from the fact that the ultimate founder and author of our faith is the Lord Jesus Christ.

The truth is, if we deny our history, we only become victims of the history we seek to escape. For example, if we deny the fact that Alexander Campbell played a powerful role in shaping our most fundamental presuppositions about the Bible and the Christian faith—if we deny that fact, we may become Campbellites with a vengeance. After all, if we deny Campbell's place in our movement, there is no way to critique or assess the very real influence he has exerted upon each of us. We cannot critique the ideas and presuppositions we have inherited from Campbell because, in effect, we pretend that Campbell did not exist. If we pretend that Campbell did not exist, we then cripple our ability either to affirm his positive contributions or to liberate ourselves from his negative contributions. The truth is, by denying our history, we allow ourselves to become ten times more the children of Alexander Campbell than we might be if we acknowledged our history honestly, candidly, and forthrightly.

The paradox is this: only when we acknowledge our history can we be freed from the constraints of our history. Only then are we freed to embrace or reject specific ideas or presuppositions that we have inherited from Campbell, Stone, and others who have placed their stamp on this movement. But if we deny our history, we are victims of a story we don't even know.

But there is more at stake here even than this. If we deny our history, we make ourselves into something we are not. We lift ourselves from the plane of ordinary mortal existence to some transcendent realm, untouched and unaffected by human experience. In effect, we make ourselves gods. If, therefore, we wish to catch a fuller glimpse of the glory, the grandeur, and the power of God, and if we wish to embrace a more realistic assessment of our own failures and limitations, there is no better way to begin than to come to terms with our own very human history.

Closely connected with this issue is our common claim that Churches of Christ do not constitute a denomination. I want to explore that claim in the light of the larger issue of the nature and meaning of God.

In the early nineteenth century, it made a great deal of sense to claim that we were not a denomination, for in a very literal and realistic sense, we simply were not. We were a movement, designed to bring all Christians into a common orbit around the principles of the first Christian age. In those days, the claim that we were not a denomination served a descriptive purpose, not a theological purpose.

In time, however, we ceased to be a movement and became a very particular organization. We had "our" churches and "our" papers, "our" lectureships and "our" preachers, "our" colleges and "our" people. Clearly, we no longer comprised a loosely constructed movement. Instead, we had become a well-defined religious organization alongside other religious organizations. Yet, we continued to claim that we were not a denomination.

What could that claim have possibly meant in that context? We must acknowledge that by the mid-nineteenth century, to claim that the Church of Christ was not a denomination was to make a theological statement, not a purely descriptive statement. In time, this claim became a theological shibboleth, an assumption that carried with it a considerable amount of theological freight. Listen, for example, to John Rogers, who argued in 1860 that members of Churches of Christ should never speak of the "other denominations." "When we speak of other *denominations*," Rogers wrote, "we place ourselves *among them*, as one of *them*. This, however, we can never do, unless we abandon the distinctive ground — the apostolic ground — the anti-sectarian ground, we have taken."[12]

Clearly, the nondenominational language was simply another way of underscoring our contention that while other churches floundered in history and tradition, we were the one true church since we had found the truth and restored the church, just as it existed in the first Christian age. Presumably, we too would become a denomination if we were to compromise biblical truth in the slightest degree. Our nondenominational status, therefore, depended on our ability to remain faithful to the apostolic ground on which we had staked our claim.

Paul underscores the theological problem with this kind of claim in Galatians 3:10: "All who rely on observing the law are under a curse, for it is written: 'Cursed is everyone who does not continue to do everything written in the Book of the Law.'" If we extrapolate from Paul's statement a meaning appropriate to our own situation in the nineteenth century, we might argue that we were under obligation to restore the ancient church in every detail, lest we become a denomination and thereby fall under judgment.

But beyond the claim that we had fully restored the ancient church, the nondenominational language carried with it other fundamental and far-reaching assumptions. Implicitly it suggested that Churches of Christ were immune to the power of history, culture, and tradition. Other religious organizations fell prey to these inexorable forces — but we did not. Other religious organizations had their vision clouded by ordinary human limitations — but we did not. Somehow, we had burst the bounds of our human constraints to achieve a perfection denied to everyone else. In effect, then, we refused to confess the depths of our own humanity, the first step toward confessing that God alone is the Living God.

---

12 John Rogers, *A Discourse Delivered in Carlisle, Kentucky, ... 1860* (Cincinnati: n.p., 1861), 22.

Surely, it is legitimate to claim that the denominational arrangement is wrong, since we know full well that Jesus prayed for the unity of all believers. But why must we claim that we do not partake of that sin? In what other areas of our lives do we claim to be sinless? What possible purpose is served when we claim perfection in this regard?

Suppose we refused to root our self-understanding in the righteousness we think we achieve when we restore the ancient church. Suppose, instead, we rooted our self-understanding in the righteousness whereby God makes us righteous, in spite of our faults and, indeed, in spite of our failure faithfully to reproduce the ancient church. If we took the righteousness of God as our starting point, would it not then make sense to make the more modest claim that because the denominational arrangement is wrong, we therefore reject it in principle? But would it not also make sense to confess that we may well partake of that sin along with everyone else? To make that confession is not to state that we willfully violate the unity of the body of Christ. Rather, to make that confession is to acknowledge that we are finite human beings, inevitably bound to certain historical and cultural structures from which we cannot extricate ourselves. One of those structures is the denominational arrangement in the United States.

Frankly, I have felt for many years that our non-denominational claims carry with them such an affirmation of perfection and such a denial of our humanity and our finitude that they effectively block us from two of the greatest gifts of the Christian faith. One such gift is the search for truth that is surely our birthright, not only as participants in the Stone-Campbell tradition, but also as members in the body of Christ. But how can we possibly keep alive a meaningful search for truth if we claim that we are not a denomination, but rather the "true Church of Christ," now restored in its fullness to the earth. The other gift is the greatest gift of all, the gift of God's grace which is the gospel of Jesus Christ. But how can we possibly hear the gospel if we are preoccupied with our own perfection?

Conclusions

In this chapter and the one before, I have sought to highlight what I take to be one of the central themes in the Stone-Campbell tradition in the early years of our movement, namely, the notion that God is God and all human beings are fallible. Alexander Campbell and Barton Stone seldom made direct and explicit statements to that effect, but they pointed unmistakably to their convictions in that regard when they spoke about truth. On the one hand, they insisted that every human being has the God-given right to search for truth. On the other, they argued that no one can possibly capture the truth, possess the truth, or codify the truth. They made these points time and again, simply because they knew that God is truth and the source of truth, and that human beings can never capture the truth of God in a creed or a system or a plan or an orthodoxy of any form, shape, or fashion.

I also argued that reforming movements dedicated to a larger vision of the truth of God often lose sight of that original goal within a few generations. This was surely the case with Lutherans, Calvinists, and Anabaptists in the sixteenth century. In Churches of Christ, however, this transformation occurred within a few short years. While Campbell and Stone had pressed for a perpetual search for truth, some in Churches of Christ claimed that the truth was now found and the search was therefore closed. And while Campbell and Stone claimed that God's truth defies codification and that restoration must therefore be an ongoing process, some among Churches of Christ began to claim that restoration was now complete. Those who made these claims subverted the very essence of the Stone-Campbell tradition.

I love this tradition, and I want to see it flourish. But I am convinced that it will flourish again only when we take seriously the fact that ours is a finite movement and not the fullness of the Kingdom of God. I am convinced that it will flourish again only when we extend to every person the unalienable right to search for truth. I am convinced that it will flourish again only when we proclaim in all of our congregations the lordship of Jesus Christ and the sovereignty of Almighty God. And I am convinced that it will flourish again when we fall on our knees and confess our failures not only as individual Christians but also as a community of believers who wear the name "the Churches of Christ." Our ability to make that confession is rooted deeply in the Stone-Campbell tradition. As John Rogers put it many years ago, "We have no reason to conclude, we know all the truth.... We have nothing to lose in this inquiry after truth. We have no system to bind us to human opinions."

*section
two*

KINGDOM

ETHICS

four

WHAT CAN WE LEARN FROM OUR HISTORY?

There are several objectives we might have in mind when we ask the question, "What can we learn from our history?" On the one hand, we might ask what we can learn about the strengths of our movement. It is certainly legitimate to ask what is right about Churches of Christ, and I have given a great deal of thought to that question over the years. There is much that is good and right about our heritage, and I explore some of those strengths in this book's very first chapter.

Now, however, I want to shift the focus in a different direction. When we ask, "What can we learn from our history?" I want to ask how we can improve. I want to know how we as a people of God can be more biblical, more faithful to the cross, and more devoted to the cause of God. I firmly believe that our history can help us answer these questions.

Some twenty years ago, when I first began work on *Reviving the Ancient Faith*, I knew relatively little about the history of Churches of Christ. But I wanted to learn about the heritage in which I had been raised, and that for me was sufficient reason to accept the invitation to write the book.

I wanted to learn more about my heritage in part because I wanted to understand myself. To say that

I was raised in Churches of Christ is an understatement. The truth is that my experience in Churches of Christ shaped and molded me in profound and inescapable ways. In a very real sense, the church was both my mother and my father. And so I agreed to write a history of Churches of Christ because I felt that if I could learn more about the heritage that had raised me, I could learn more about who I was and why.

I had many questions to which I wanted answers, all of which grew from my own experience in Churches of Christ. But none of my questions were more important to me than why Churches of Christ took so little interest in social ethics. Why, for example, were we so reluctant to see the implications the gospel holds for large-scale issues of peace and justice? Why were we so reluctant for so many years to confront the issue of racial segregation? And perhaps most pressing for me when I first undertook to write this book: why did Churches of Christ take so little interest in the great moral issues that convulsed the country during those turbulent years of the 1960s?

These were questions that, at least in part, gave shape to the book, *Reviving the Ancient Faith*, because these were questions that for fourteen years I almost daily asked of Alexander Campbell, of Barton Stone, of David Lipscomb, of J. N. Armstrong, of George Benson, of Reuel Lemmons, and a host of other luminaries in our heritage.

The Gospel, Public Policy & Social Issues

For most of my life, my experience in Churches of Christ has been supportive. I especially treasure my memories of church during my childhood and adolescence, thanks to some wonderful Texas congregations that nurtured and sustained me during those pivotal years. Those churches included Broadway in Lubbock, Skillman Avenue in Dallas, and Johnson Street in San Angelo. In every instance, those were great churches whose preachers and Bible class teachers taught me the Bible, explained the love of God and the cross of Christ, and held out for me a model for Christian living. During all those years, I never heard one word about the premillennial controversy or the anti-institutional controversy—or any other controversy or fight, for that matter. The seamy side of Churches of Christ was simply not a part of my upbringing.

It was not until the late 1960s that I found myself disillusioned with certain aspects of my heritage. The crisis I endured had nothing to do with pre-millennialism, anti-ism, or sectarianism. Instead, it had everything to do with our failure to connect the gospel with the culture in which we lived.

I was a graduate student during those years at the University of Iowa. The country was aflame with some of the greatest moral issues in the history of the United States: the legitimacy of America's role in the Vietnam War and the question of equal rights for all Americans, white and black. The university community—my world at the time—was alive in those days with passionate debate and even with boisterous demonstrations. No one I knew thought these issues inconsequential. To the contrary, they dominated conversation in almost every setting, from the classroom to the local pizza parlor.

Ironically, these questions seldom surfaced during my undergraduate years at one of our Christian colleges. But now, on the campus of a major state university, these were questions I found I could not avoid. Almost instinctively, I measured them by the biblical principles I had learned as a boy in those Texas churches many years ago. Based on those principles, it didn't take me long to decide that these were indeed moral issues to which the gospel spoke with clarity and force. I couldn't picture the Prince of Peace waging any war, especially this war. And I couldn't picture Jesus discriminating against people on the basis of their color or their race. And so I involved myself in these issues, not as a radical or a subversive—not even as a partisan of a particular political party—but as a Christian, attempting to put into practice what I felt I had learned about the gospel many years ago.

But then, as I read the various gospel papers that came to our little apartment in Iowa City, I discovered that my understanding of the gospel—the one I had learned as a boy—stood somehow light-years removed from judgments on these issues offered by most of the leaders of our churches. Quite simply, they thought these issues unrelated to the gospel.

This point hit me with particular force in 1970. I was only a year away from finishing my doctoral work at Iowa, and several colleges related to Churches of Christ had invited me to interview for teaching positions. I accepted those invitations and made a single whirlwind tour, exploring job possibilities at schools in New Mexico, Texas, and Tennessee. In the middle of one of those interviews, I learned of a tragedy that had taken place earlier that day—a tragedy that would ripple through the nation and through the psyches of thousands of young people in the United States with devastating effect for months and even years to come. It was May 4—a day I remember well. Students all over the United States had launched massive demonstrations on that day to protest our nation's incursion into Cambodia. One of those protests took place at Kent State University in Ohio. Suddenly, without warning, some of the young National Guardsmen patrolling the campus panicked and fired into the crowd. Four Kent State students fell to the ground, shot to death.

Several hours later and hundreds of miles further south, I was immersed in a job interview at one of our schools. The man conducting the interview—a professor and a highly influential figure among Churches of Christ—informed me of those killings, clearly seeking to gauge my response. I was stunned, no doubt visibly so, and before I could say a word, the professor suddenly turned to me and said, "If you're one of those troublemakers, we don't need you here."

This sort of response to the great moral issues of those years characterized many in Churches of Christ. In fact, the most prominent gospel papers in our fellowship typically responded to the Civil Rights Movement and the Vietnam War in two ways. First—and most often—they greeted these events with a deafening silence that loudly proclaimed their conviction that these issues were fundamentally unrelated to the gospel. Second, they sometimes cast their lot with the forces of law and order that sought to subdue the voices of dissent. Almost never did white, mainstream Churches of Christ support the great, swelling movement on behalf of peace and justice that captured the imaginations of so many Americans during those years.

The failure of my own church to connect the gospel to these important moral issues raised for me a simple but very powerful question: Why? Why did most of us refuse to engage the issues of those years, and why did we not see that the gospel speaks to questions of justice and peace just as surely as it speaks of baptism, worship, and salvation?

The most obvious answer to that question lies in the fact that while we are Christians, we are also creatures of the culture in which we live.

In the World & Of the World

A brief story will help us see the implications of this point. When my mother was eleven or twelve years old, the older people in the church reminded all the children that Christians are to be "peculiar" people. When my mother looked at herself, she couldn't see that she was especially peculiar at all, but knowing what she had been told, she went out of her way—at least for a period in her life—to be as peculiar as possible.

This story can help us see that while we desperately want to embrace the values of the kingdom of God, we sometimes embrace little more than the values of our culture. We sometimes sanctify those values with church attendance and pious rhetoric, then confuse those values with the values of the Christian faith. In this way, it is easy for otherwise good and faithful Christians to be not only in the world but also *of* the world.

Because it is always easier to see a particular failing in others instead of in ourselves, it might be helpful to take as an example for our study the millions of white Americans during the seventeenth, eighteenth, and nineteenth centuries who claimed to be faithful followers of Jesus but who found themselves inextricably wed to the institution of slavery. Black Americans—both slave and free—easily saw what those white Americans could not see, namely, that the religion professed by many white Americans was not Christianity at all, but rather a creation of their culture which they sanctified by involvement in their churches.

While virtually all the slave narratives make this point, no book from that period is more explicit in this regard than the *Narrative of the Life of Frederick Douglass*, written in 1845. In an eloquent passage, Douglass charged that

> between the Christianity of this land, and the Christianity of Christ, I recognize the widest possible difference—so wide, that to receive the one as good, pure, and holy, is of necessity to reject the other as bad, corrupt, and wicked. To be the friend of the one, is of necessity to be the enemy of the other. I love the pure, peaceable, and impartial Christianity of Christ: I therefore hate the corrupt, slaveholding, women-whipping, cradle-plundering, partial and hypocritical Christianity of this land. Indeed, I can see no reason, but the most deceitful one, for

calling the religion of this land Christianity. I look upon it as the climax of all misnomers, the boldest of all frauds, and the grossest of all libels.[1]

Then, recognizing that a host of American Christians, both northern and southern, either actively supported the institution of slavery or refused to condemn it boldly, Douglass concluded, "Dark and terrible as is this picture, I hold it to be strictly true of the overwhelming mass of professed Christians in America."[2]

We must now ask, have we in Churches of Christ accommodated ourselves to the culture in which we live in similar ways? If we are honest, we must confess that yes, there have been times when we have. The fact that for many years we allowed the cultural constraints of the American South to determine our posture on race relations is only the most obvious case in point.

How else should we understand G. C. Brewer's report that when he was a boy in Tennessee in the early twentieth century, "None of us thought of inviting Negroes into our homes as guests or of sitting down to eat with them at the same table; we felt, as a matter of course, that they should have the same food that we ate, but that they should eat in the kitchen or in the servants' quarters"? According to Brewer, "This was the condition that prevailed and this we accepted as right and satisfactory."[3]

How else should we understand Howard White's report regarding the great African-American evangelist, Marshall Keeble? During the five years that White taught at David Lipscomb College, Keeble "came every year to speak at the lectures. Not once

---

1 Frederick Douglass, *Narrative of the Life of Frederick Douglass*, 1845 (New York: Signet Books, 1968), 120.

2 Ibid., 123.

3 G. C. Brewer, "Saved By a Moonbeam; or, Facing Death for Saying a Negro Has a Soul," unpublished paper, 2–3.

was he invited to join a luncheon or a dinner or to do anything else beyond speaking. His students and associates from the Nashville Christian Institute were segregated in one corner of the balcony."[4]

How else should we understand the recommendation of Foy Wallace, Jr. for what he viewed as the proper relationship between white preachers and black church members? Wallace reported that

> when N.B. Hardeman held the valley-wide meeting at Harlingen, Texas, some misguided brethren brought a group of negroes up to the front to be introduced to and shake hands with him. Brother Hardeman told them publicly that he could see all of the colored brethren he cared to see on the outside after services, and that he could say everything to them he wanted to say without the formality of shaking hands.[5]

Or again, how else should we understand Wallace's statement that an acceptable black preacher is one who "knows what his relationships are in the church in the light of his relationships with society."[6]

Finally, how else should we understand the fact that colleges related to Churches of Christ admitted black students long after most other institutions in the South had taken this step? In this regard, black evangelist R.N. Hogan, editor of the *Christian Echo*, the gospel paper that had served African-American Churches of Christ since 1902, leveled a devastating critique against the segregated colleges in our fellowship. Interestingly, Hogan's critique in 1960 sounded very much like Frederick Douglass's critique of American Christianity in 1845. Douglass claimed, we recall, that he could "see no reason,

---

4 Howard A. White, letter to Reuel Lemmons, June 10, 1968.

5 Foy Wallace Jr., "Negro Meetings for White People," *Bible Banner* 3 (March 1941): 7.

6 Wallace, addendum to Keeble, "From M. Keeble," *Bible Banner* 3 (April 1941), 5.

but the most deceitful one, for calling the religion of this land Christianity. I look upon it as the climax of all misnomers, the boldest of all frauds, and the grossest of all libels." Hogan said much the same of those colleges among Churches of Christ that resisted integration for so long. Those who ran the schools that refused to admit African-American students, Hogan demanded, should "stop calling themselves Christians, stop calling their schools Christian schools, and stop calling their churches, churches of Christ."[7] For Hogan, it was that simple.

We can certainly respond to charges like those of Frederick Douglass and R. N. Hogan by dismissing them as sheer propaganda, as overstatement, as nothing more than highly charged rhetoric designed to win points in a political struggle. But if we take this course, we will never see that Douglass and Hogan were seeking to communicate what they regarded as bedrock, biblical truths. First, they called us to see that the gospel does have social and political implications. This is something that African-American Christians have known for four hundred years. Second, they called us to see that in many ways, white churches had allowed themselves to become so shaped and molded by the values of the larger culture that they were no longer Christian in any meaningful sense.

If we have ears to hear, Douglass and Hogan can help us to understand how easily Christians can succumb to the dictates of our culture, in spite of the fact that those dictates may run absolutely counter to the clear word of God. And so, if we ask why Churches of Christ were so reluctant in the 1960s to discern how the gospel connects to the cause of peace or the cause of justice for the poor and the

---

7   R. N. Hogan, "Brother David Lipscomb Stood with God on Race Prejudice in the Church of Christ," *Christian Echo* 55 (June 1960): 2.

oppressed, one answer must certainly be that we had found a comfortable niche in the American South and, for the most part, simply followed the lead of the culture in which we lived.

It does little good to explore the kind of history we have explored here unless we also ask about the implications of that history for our lives and for our churches in the world of the twenty-first century. None of us wants to take our cues from the culture. Each of us wants to take our cues from the gospel. And yet, we have seen that cultural values can be seductive and that we can be seduced in spite of our noblest intentions to be faithful to the mandates of God. In the following chapter, therefore, I want to explore some of the resources inherent in our own movement that can help us to guard against the kind of cultural accommodationism that we have described here.

f i v e

RESISTING THE SIRENS
OF CULTURE

We saw in the previous chapter how easily Christians can be seduced by the values of the culture in which we live. I want to ask now, "How can we guard against this kind of seduction?"

The truth is, we have at our disposal two powerful antidotes against cultural accommodation, both of which are rooted deeply in the heritage of Churches of Christ. These two include 1) the restoration ideal that has been central to our history and identity from the beginning and 2) an apocalyptic worldview that was important to Churches of Christ, especially in the nineteenth century. I would like to explore each of these in turn.

The Restoration Ideal

I am keenly aware that the restoration ideal is rapidly losing its currency among Churches of Christ. Many feel—based on their reading of our history for the past two hundred years—that the restoration ideal has spawned arrogance and division and little else. There is surely justification for that perspective. After all, one who claims to restore the ancient Christian faith often suggests that he or she cannot find that faith in any fellowship on earth that claims the name Christian. For this

67

reason, restorationists often turn out to be radical separatists, rejecting other Christian denominations as un- or even anti-Christian. Further, within the framework of restoration movements, there are always some who feel that their restored church has missed some key point in the ancient Christian tradition. Those who feel this way often proceed to divide from the original restorationist fellowship and launch yet another sect committed to the restoration of the ancient order. We in Churches of Christ are all too familiar with these aspects of the restorationist heritage.

And yet, for all of its liabilities, I want to suggest that the restoration vision is intrinsically valuable and that if we in Churches of Christ relinquish that vision, we will do so at our own peril. I say this based on one fundamental consideration: the restoration vision is finally nothing more than a tool that allows us to take our bearings from the first Christian age. It allows us to discriminate between human traditions and the divine will. It allows us to ask if such and such a practice or doctrine or perspective is really authorized by scripture, or only by some human system devised at some point along the path of Christian history. Surely, there can be nothing wrong with a tool that always points us to the founding tradition of the Christian faith. Based on that realization, the restoration vision can be of enormous help to us as we seek to resist the seductions of our culture.

But has it helped? The answer to that question does not depend on the legitimacy of the restoration principle itself. Rather, it depends on how we have employed that principle.

In that context, it is helpful to think of the restoration principle as a powerful searchlight that will illumine any aspect of scripture on which we shine its beam. If we shine it on the Sermon on the Mount, it will illumine the Sermon on the Mount. If we shine it on Acts 2, it will illumine Acts 2. If we shine

it on Romans 8, it will illumine Romans 8. To carry
out our analogy, then, it is obvious that in addition
to the restoration searchlight, another key factor is
the person who guides and directs that searchlight.
In other words, how do we decide how we will use
the searchlight of the restoration principle?

For most of our history, the driving force behind
our use of the restoration searchlight has been a
philosophical perspective properly known as
Scottish Common Sense Realism, but popularly
known as Baconianism. Baconianism originated
in the eighteenth century in response to radical
thinkers who suggested that human beings have
no direct knowledge of objects or events outside
themselves. Instead, these thinkers argued, all we
can know is our perception of those objects or
events. This raised the very critical question of the
extent to which we can know with certainty anything
outside ourselves at all.

To this question, the Scottish Common Sense
Baconians essentially said, "Hogwash. Common
sense tells us that we can know objects outside
ourselves with absolute certainty. When the farmer
plows his field, does he question whether he is using
a plow or a horse or whether he is really working
in the dirt? Of course not. He knows those things
with certainty, and the fact that he knows that he
knows enables him to plow his field both effectively
and confidently."

Having made that claim, the Scottish Baconians
then explained how we can always know with certainty the nature of the world that lies outside
ourselves. The key, they argued, is the scientific
method, devised by Francis Bacon in the seventeenth century. According to that method, one does
not begin with one's biases and then collect data in
order to prove what one has already determined.
That is to put the cart before the horse. Rather, one
begins by collecting data, and only when there is
adequate data does one draw a conclusion. The

point is, our conclusions must always be based on data, and not the other way around.

The beauty of the Baconian method was that it did enable people to know the world outside of themselves with certainty. And because it enabled people to know with certainty, it enabled them to agree with one another. After all, when scientific experiments tell us that water is composed of two parts of hydrogen and one part of oxygen, how many people will argue over that conclusion? Or, when the data confirms that gravity pulls objects toward the earth, how many people want to contend over that issue?

It was precisely here that our forefathers, especially Alexander Campbell, found the Baconian method useful even in religion. The greatest problem Campbell faced on the nineteenth-century American frontier was the propensity of Christians to divide and subdivide because they couldn't agree over the various fine points of the Christian faith. But then it occurred to Campbell, what if Christians could approach the Bible from the perspective of the scientific method? If Christians, for example, had a question about a particular doctrine, could they not search the Bible for all the data that pertained to that doctrine, put the data on the table, analyze it, and draw the correct conclusions? If Christians could proceed in such a scientific fashion, would they not inevitably agree? And would not that agreement finally overcome the divisions that plagued Christendom, uniting all Christians around a common platform, rooted in a scientific worldview?

Perhaps the best example of the scientific method at work in our own movement is the way we commonly construct what we call the "plan of salvation." As we know, there is no single verse in Scripture that lines out the "plan of salvation" as we teach it, namely, that the convert must hear, believe, repent, confess, and be baptized. Instead, we typically find a verse here that speaks of baptism, another there that speaks of hearing and believing, still another that speaks of confession, another that speaks of believing and repenting, and yet another that speaks of believing and being baptized. Once we have located all these verses, we put them on the table, analyze them, and finally formulate our conclusions—what we call the "plan of salvation."

We need to see that in our heritage, the Baconian method *is* the person who operates the searchlight of the restoration principle and who determines the objects on which the light will shine. And what are the objects which that light will illumine? The Baconian method predetermines that the restoration searchlight will focus its beam on biblical facts and data. Alexander Campbell made this point abundantly clear: "The Bible is a book of facts," he contended, "not of opinions, theories, abstract generalities, nor of verbal definitions.... The meaning of the Bible facts is the true biblical doctrine."[1] And the task of the biblical interpreter is to approach the Bible as if it were a scientific manual, always analyzing its teaching with the aid of the scientific method. Accordingly, Campbell argued that the "inductive style of inquiring and reasoning, is to be as rigidly carried out in reading and teaching the Bible facts and documents, as in the analysis and synthesis of physical nature."[2]

It is no wonder, then, that for much of our history, we have focused the searchlight of the restoration principle almost exclusively on biblical materials that describe the forms and structures of the ancient church. This is precisely why we finally began using the concept of *blueprint*: we approach the Bible as if we were scientists, or perhaps architectural engineers, seeking to reconstruct an ancient blueprint, and once we have that blueprint in place, we seek to reconstruct the ancient building.

---

1 Alexander Campbell, *The Christian System*, 1835 (Cincinnati: Standard Publishing Co., 1901), 6.

2 Campbell, "Schools and Colleges—No. 2," *Millennial Harbinger*, 3d ser., 7 (March 1850): 172.

Yet—and this is the critical point of this chapter—if we have any serious expectation that the restoration vision will help us resist the seductions of our culture, then we must train the restoration spotlight on biblical materials that deal with ethics and questions of Christian lifestyle.

Put another way, if we use the restoration vision only to help us determine that the early church employed a plurality of both elders and deacons, or that the early church partook of the Lord's supper on every first day of the week, or that the early church did not use instrumental music in worship—if this is the extent of our use of the restoration principle, then surely we cannot expect that principle to lend us much help with our efforts to resist the seductions and allurements of our culture. Yet, by now it must be clear that so long as the Baconian method, in effect, is the person who operates the restoration searchlight, that light will inevitably focus its beam on facts, data, blueprints, and architectural details, and will seldom if ever illumine what Jesus called the "weightier matters of the law."

An Apocalyptic Worldview

And so, we now must ask, are there alternatives? Is there a way to redirect the restoration searchlight to illumine biblical materials that can nurture and sustain us as we seek to resist the seductions of our culture?

Thankfully, the answer to that question is a resounding "yes," and the alternative I wish to explore belongs fully as much to the heritage of Churches of Christ as does the Baconian method of biblical interpretation.

The alternative I have in mind is what I called in *Reviving the Ancient Faith* an "apocalyptic worldview." When I use that term, I do not have in mind the violent introduction of the Kingdom of God, or even the premillennial rule of Christ on earth for a thousand years, though I know that some people associate the term "apocalyptic" with both of those concepts. Rather, when I use the phrase "apocalyptic worldview," I have in mind a way of viewing the world—and living in the world—from the perspective of the coming Kingdom of God. Put another way, one who holds to an apocalyptic orientation takes very seriously the promise of the end of this age and the assurance that the Kingdom of God will finally triumph. But more than that, he or she seeks to live his or her life *as if* the final triumph of the Kingdom of God were complete. For one who subscribes to this perspective, the Kingdom of God is not something far off in the future. Rather, the Kingdom of God is the defining presence, the only reality that matters. Ultimately, all else is illusion.

What would it mean if we lived our lives from this perspective, if we walked—as one book puts it—in "the shadow of the second coming"? Would our priorities be different from what they are today? Would our goals and ambitions be transformed? What difference would it make if you sought to live your life *as if* the final rule of God were fully present in the here and now?

One thing we must say about the apocalyptic worldview is this: it provides us with an entirely different perspective on reality from the perspective fostered by Scottish Common Sense Baconianism. If we view the world through the lens of Scottish Common Sense Baconianism, we view the world through the lens of the mundane, through the lens of the earthly, through the lens of the merely scientific. But if we view the world from an apocalyptic perspective, we view it through the lens of the coming Kingdom of God. The difference between the two could not be more dramatic.

At first glance, someone might object to this comparison on the grounds that it pits apples against oranges. After all, Scottish Common Sense Realism—at least in the context of our movement—is a hermeneutical principle, a way of reading the Bible;

while the apocalyptic orientation is a perspective on life. But this is just the point we must grasp: we need a way of reading the Bible that is at one and the same time our fundamental life perspective or worldview. Otherwise, we run the risk of disconnecting the Bible from the main issues of our lives.

It is certainly true that the Baconian hermeneutic can also serve us as a worldview or life principle. But do we really wish to embrace a worldview that is little more than the scientific method? Is this really what life is all about? Flesh ... and blood ... and dust of the earth? Or is life—from a Christian perspective—finally about living in the context of the Kingdom of God? And if we conclude that authentic life—full, rich, and abundant life—has its beginning and end in the Kingdom of God, then would it not make sense to allow that conviction to serve also as our hermeneutical principle?

And so we return to the question: what difference would it make if we read the Bible from the perspective of the coming Kingdom of God? I can tell you that it made a great deal of difference to many in Churches of Christ throughout the nineteenth century and even well into the twentieth century. In the context of our movement, Barton Stone, one of the two most important leaders of Churches of Christ in the early nineteenth century, is the fountainhead of this perspective. Because of his apocalyptic orientation, Stone embraced a life of radical discipleship. He downplayed material concerns and geared his life to ethical and moral commitments in the light of the coming Kingdom of God. He avoided extravagant attire, ministered to the poor and the hungry, and freed the slaves that came into his possession by virtue of his marriage to a Tennessee woman. He called on his followers to open their lives to the Holy Spirit and, in the power of the Spirit, to abandon self for the sake of others, to render aid to those in need, and to stand with those who suffered. If Campbell found in scripture models for the worship and organization of the church, Stone found in scripture models for holy living. He summed up the direction of his life when he urged in 1842, "No Christian lives for himself—not self but the Lord is the great end of his living.... Like an obedient servant, he says, Lord what wilt thou have me to do? And when that will is known, he flies to do [it], not regarding how great the sacrifice of wealth, ease, or reputation."[3] If there is a single verse that characterized the life and work of Stone, surely it is Romans 12:2: "Be not conformed to this world, but be ye transformed by the renewing of your minds."

More than any other nineteenth- or twentieth-century leader of our movement, David Lipscomb inherited Barton Stone's apocalyptic perspective. Lipscomb spelled out that perspective in substantial detail in a little book he wrote in 1889 simply called *Civil Government*. If one doubts that the apocalyptic orientation stood at the center of Lipscomb's thought, one need only hear Lipscomb's own appraisal of this book: "Nothing we ever wrote affects so nearly the vital interests of the church of Christ and the salvation of the world as this little book." And regarding the apocalyptic vision he elaborated in that book, he wrote that these themes were the very "key notes ... of the Old and New Testaments" and that without them, the Bible was "without point or meaning."[4]

The pressing question for us is this: what difference did Lipscomb's apocalyptic orientation make for the way he lived his daily life? Answers are not hard to find. We get an early clue from the old restoration preacher Benjamin Franklin who reported

---

3 Barton W. Stone, "Christian Expositor," *Christian Messenger* 12 (July 1842): 272.

4 David Lipscomb, "Religion and Politics," *Gospel Advocate* 32 (26 March 1890): 199; and *Civil Government* (Nashville: Gospel Advocate, 1889), 25, 27–8, and 96.

in 1875 that Lipscomb was "a plain and unassuming man, with the simplicity of a child.... He lives in utter disregard of the notions of the world, puts on no airs, [and] wears just a coat, hat and pants as suit him."[5]

When Lipscomb, armed with his apocalyptic vision, spoke of separation from the world, he did not mean mere morality. He had not the slightest doubt that "the devil is willing to turn moral reformer and make the world moral and respectable." Rather, Lipscomb called for "a full surrender of the soul, mind, and body up to God," leading to "the spirit of self-denial, of self-sacrifice, the forbearance [*sic*] and long suffering, [and] the doing good for evil."[6]

One finds an especially notable example of the spirit of self-denial to which Lipscomb was committed when a cholera epidemic struck Nashville in 1873. During the month of June alone, almost 500 people died. Blacks were especially hard hit. Many who had the means to flee the city did so. Lipscomb was not well and had every reason to escape the plague by retiring to his farm at Bell's Bend, outside the city. Lipscomb believed, however, that his citizenship in the Kingdom of God required him to go into houses where the plague had struck, to clean and feed the victims, and to do everything in his power to help restore their health. He urged Churches of Christ in Nashville to follow suit. "It is a time that should call out the full courage and energy of the church in looking after the needy," he wrote. "Every individual, black or white, that dies from neglect and want of proper food and nursing, is a reproach to the professors of the Christian religion in the vicinity of Nashville."[7]

---

5   Benjamin Franklin, "Visit to Tennessee," *American Christian* Review 13 (July 1875): 220.

6   Lipscomb, *Civil Government*, 144–5, 133.

7   Lipscomb, "The Cholera," *Gospel Advocate* 15 (26 June 1873): 619.

Like Barton Stone and Tolbert Fanning before him, Lipscomb also committed himself to a life of rigorous pacifism, a commitment that reflected his devotion to the Kingdom of God as opposed to human governments. "All human government," he wrote, "rests for authority upon the power of the sword." In contrast, the Kingdom of God was a realm of peace. How, then, Lipscomb wondered, could a Christian participate in acts of violence? In 1881, Lipscomb contrasted the brutality that characterized human governments with the spirit of peace that ruled the Kingdom of God.

> In the beginning of the late strife that so fearfully desolated our country, much was said about "our enemies." I protested that I had not a single enemy, and was not an enemy to a single man North of the Ohio river.... Yet,... thousands and hundreds of thousands who knew not each other... were made enemies to each other and thrown into fierce and bloody strife, were embued with the spirit of destruction one toward the other, through the instrumentality of human governments.[8]

As a final measure of Lipscomb's commitment to countercultural values, we should note his consistent bias toward and concern for the poor. In fact, Lipscomb thought that poverty was a fundamental characteristic of the Kingdom of God. In his judgment, the church was "the especial legacy of God to the poor of the earth.... It is the rich that are out of their element in Christ's Church." In 1906, he confirmed this judgment when he argued that "Christ intended his religion for the poor, [and] adapted it to their necessities."[9]

---

8   Lipscomb, "Babylon," *Gospel Advocate* 23 (2 June 1881): 340.

9   Lipscomb, *Gospel Advocate* 8 (27 February 1866): 141; and "Tolbert Fanning's Teaching and Influence" in James E. Scobey, ed., *Franklin College and Its Influences* (Nashville: McQuiddy Printing, 1906), 59–60.

It would be easy enough to argue that Lipscomb's devotion to the poor was nothing more than a function of his own meager circumstances—if only that were true. In point of fact, Lipscomb inherited substantial means from a moderately wealthy father. David Lipscomb, for whatever reason, was a man driven by his vision of the coming Kingdom of God—a kingdom that would someday rule with righteousness and justice over all the earth and that would finally destroy human governments along with popular values based on self-indulgence. Lipscomb therefore committed himself to live *as if* that kingdom were present in the here and now. This was his apocalyptic worldview.

Conclusions

This perspective—this commitment to live our lives as if the Kingdom of God were fully present in the here and now—can shine the searchlight of the restoration vision on biblical materials that Scottish Common Sense rationalism can hardly illumine at all. Instead of assuming that the Bible is a divinely-given scientific treatise, the apocalyptic perspective assumes that the Bible is a narrative that tells the story of a God who created us from the dust of the earth, who loves us and redeemed us when we went astray, who calls us to reflect his love to others just as he has loved us, and who one day will triumph over all the earth and rule for ever and ever. These two perspectives, then—Baconianism and apocalypticism—offer us two competing hermeneutics, that is, two very different ways of reading the Bible. We want to explore in the next chapter how those two different hermeneutics can virtually determine how Christians should respond to social and ethical issues.

THE BIBLE & ETHICAL ISSUES

I suggested in the previous chapter that the restoration principle is a powerful searchlight that will illumine any aspect of scripture on which we shine its beam. If we shine the beam on Acts 2, it will illumine Acts 2. If we shine the beam on Romans 8, it will illumine Romans 8. And if we shine it on the teachings of Jesus in the Gospels, it will illumine those teachings.

We called the other principle an "apocalyptic worldview." One who takes this perspective seriously reads the Bible not as a collection of facts or a scientific treatise, but as a narrative or a story. After all, one who takes seriously the apocalyptic outlook discerns in the Bible a narrative of the mighty acts of God, beginning with the creation and concluding with his final triumph over all the earth.

If we ask how these two hermeneutical principles have worked themselves out in the history of our movement, the answers are not hard to find. The Baconian hermeneutic generates among our people three assumptions. First, it dictates that we should read the Bible as if it were a scientific text, looking for facts and data on the basis of which we can reconstruct the blueprint of the ancient church. Second, we find the appropriate data in commands, examples, and necessary inferences. And finally, the Baconian hermeneutic renders the

Bible essentially flat. That is, it provides us with no basis for distinguishing between central ideas and themes in the Bible and notions of lesser significance. For example, in the light of the Baconian perspective, there is no way to determine which is more important: the death, burial, and resurrection of Christ on the one hand, or the question of instrumental music on the other. Both are simply data that must be incorporated into the blueprint of the ancient Christian faith.

On the other hand, an apocalyptic perspective focuses on God's mighty deeds, culminating in his final triumph over all the earth. The focus here is on God: what he has already done for us and what he will do in the future. From the outset, then, the apocalyptic worldview determines that certain things are of first importance, and certain things are not. Of first importance is what *God* has done for us. This perspective allows us, therefore, to take seriously Paul's statement in 1 Corinthians 15:4: "For what I received, I passed on to you as of first importance: that Christ died for our sins according to the Scriptures, that he was buried, [and] that he was raised on the third day according to the Scriptures...." Further, those things Paul thought were of first importance have enormous ethical implications, for if Christ died for us, then we in turn must "offer our bodies as living sacrifices" (Romans 12:1) in imitation of our Master and in service to the neighbor. Finally, this is precisely the kind of lifestyle that makes sense in the context of the coming Kingdom of God.

Put another way, if the Baconian method inevitably focuses on biblical facts and data, the apocalyptic perspective inevitably focuses on great biblical themes that stand as corollaries to the one theme that is central to all of Scripture: the sovereignty of God. What are those themes? Creation. Redemption. Discipleship. Salvation. Perhaps there is no single passage that summarizes all those themes more completely than 2 Corinthians 5:17-19: "Therefore, if anyone is in Christ, he is a new creation; the old has gone, the new has come! All this is from God, who reconciled us to himself through Christ."

Two Hermeneutic Approaches & the Question of Slavery

It will be helpful for us to ask how these two hermeneutic principles actually played themselves out in the context of our movement when specific ethical issues were at stake. But first—just as we did in chapter four—I want once again to consider an ethical issue that is far removed from the world in which we live today and therefore one we can discuss without feeling threatened: the issue of slavery.

Those in our movement who embraced an apocalyptic worldview resolutely condemned the institution of slavery. Long before most southerners were willing even to consider emancipation, Barton Stone and those who followed his lead freed their slaves on the grounds that slavery is incompatible with the Kingdom of God. For example, when Joseph Thomas traveled in Tennessee and Kentucky in 1810-1811, he reported that

> the Christian companies in this settlement and about Cane Ridge have been large; but within a few years, many of them, who held black people as slaves, emancipated them, and have moved to the state of Ohio. I will observe that the Christians in these parts *abhor* the idea of *slavery*, and some of them have almost tho't that they who hold to slavery cannot be a Christian.[1]

Many years later in 1878, David Lipscomb learned about a congregation in McKinney, Texas that refused a black man membership. Lipscomb's response to that travesty is worth quoting in full.

---

1 Joseph Thomas, *The Travels and Gospel Labors of Joseph Thomas* (Winchester, VA: n.p., 1812), 56.

> We believe it sinful to have two congrega-
> tions in the same community for persons of
> separate and distinct races now....
> God saves the negro equally with the white
> man when he believes in Christ and puts him
> on by being buried with him in baptism.... I
> had as soon think of the worst blasphemer in
> the land, steeped in the vilest of crimes being
> saved as a man or woman who would stand
> between that individual [the Negro] and his
> obedience to God. He sets at defiance God's
> law, assumes to be greater than God, and is
> guilty of a presumptuous sin in the sight of
> God, for which we can hardly believe pardon
> can be found.... How dare a church toler-
> ate the persistent exhibition of such a spirit?
> Such a church certainly forfeits its claim to
> be a church of God....
> We mean simply this, a church which
> cannot bring an individual to see his rebel-
> lion against God in such a course, ought to
> withdraw from that individual as one who with
> a heart full of pride, bitterness and treason
> fights against God. For our part, we would
> much prefer membership with an humble
> and despised band of ignorant negroes, than
> with a congregation of the [most] aristocratic
> and refined whites in the land, cherishing
> such a spirit of defiance of God and his law,
> and all the principles of his holy religion.[2]

It is important to note that in this text, Lipscomb
makes rejection of racism a defining issue for authentic Christian faith. Accordingly, he 1) doubts whether
a racist can be saved, 2) calls for congregations to
excommunicate those who sought to refuse membership to Christians of other races, and 3) argues that a
church that tolerates racism was simply not a Church
of Christ. In making this latter point, Lipscomb stood
shoulder to shoulder with Frederick Douglass and
R. N. Hogan, two black men from two different centuries who vociferously claimed that racist churches
were not Christian churches at all.

---

2 David Lipscomb, "Race Prejudice," *Gospel Advocate* 20
   (21 February 1878): 120-1.

On the other hand, when we turn from those who embraced an apocalyptic worldview to those whose reading of the biblical text was defined primarily by a Baconian perspective, we find a radically different perspective on slavery. Alexander Campbell provides us with a notable case in point. As we have seen, Campbell sought to facilitate the unity of all Christians by holding up the Bible as a divinely given instruction manual and the gospel as a system of facts. Viewing the Bible in this way, Campbell typically downplayed questions of social justice since he could find for those questions no clearly stated biblical instructions. Because he could not fit these sorts of issues into his "blueprint" for the church, he viewed these kinds of questions as "matters of opinion," not "matters of faith."

Presumably, if Campbell had found a single passage in the New Testament that commanded, "Thou shalt not hold slaves," he would have resisted slavery on biblical grounds. But there was no such text. Campbell did reject slavery, but not because it was immoral or unchristian. Rather, he rejected slavery because "in this age and in this country it is not expedient." Put another way, he thought slavery was "not favorable to individual and national prosperity." But as far as the moral issue was concerned, Campbell wrote, "There is not one verse in the Bible inhibiting it, but many regulating it. It is not, then, we conclude, *immoral.*" In fact, Campbell argued that "in certain cases and conditions," slavery might be "morally right."[3]

On the eve of the Civil War, the crusty old Indiana preacher, Benjamin Franklin, advanced the same kind of argument regarding slavery and

---

3 Alexander Campbell, "Our Position to American Slavery—No. VIII," *Millennial Harbinger*, 3d ser., 2 (June 1845): 258-9, 263; and "Our Position to American Slavery—No. V," *Millennial Harbinger*, 3d ser., 2 (May 1845): 193.

rooted that argument squarely in his perception of the New Testament as a rulebook or blueprint.

1. If those who labor on the subject [of slavery] will show where the Lord ever gave a decision or opinion, we will publish and maintain it.
2. The same goes for the Apostles.
3. If they will show where the Lord or the Apostles ever discussed the subject, we will discuss it.
4. If they didn't discuss it, we won't.
5. Those who condemn us for ignoring it condemn Jesus and the Apostles. We follow them.[4]

The truth is, it would be very difficult for anyone to argue against slavery if the Bible is nothing more than a blueprint or a divinely given rulebook. In fact, Peter Gomes in *The Good Book* argues that if one views the Bible as a rulebook, "it would not be hard, even today, to make a biblical case for slavery. Nowhere does the Bible condemn it; everywhere in the Bible it is the practice."[5]

Gomes explains that everywhere in the antebellum South, white southerners intent on defending slavery did so by treating the Bible as a blueprint. For example—and here I quote from Gomes directly—

> When in 1856 the Reverend Thornton Stringfellow, a Virginia Baptist, published his sermon "A Scriptural View of Slavery," he argued that God himself had sanctioned slavery through Noah, Abraham, and Joseph, and that the biblical record was unambiguous. When a convention of Confederate ministers in Richmond Virginia, in April 1863, published their "Address to Christians throughout the World," making the case for the morality of the Confederate cause as Christians,

---

4 Benjamin Franklin, "Our Position Called For," *American Christian Review* 2 (March 1859): 42, cited by James Brooks Major in "The Role of Periodicals in the Development of the Disciples of Christ, 1850–1910" (Ph.D. diss., Vanderbilt University, 1966), 97.

5 Peter J. Gomes, *The Good Book* (New York: William Morrow and Co., 1996), 89.

they...argued that "the practicable plan for benefiting the African race must be the Providential plan—the Scriptural plan."[6]

Gomes then explains that "in order to make their biblical position clear," the ministers based their case on I Timothy 6:1-2, "where the Apostle instructs the young minister of Jesus on the subject of slavery."

> Let as many servants as are under the yoke count their own masters worthy of all honor that the name of God and his doctrine be not blasphemed. And they that have believing masters, let them not despise them because they are brethren; but rather do them service because they are faithful and beloved, partakers of the benefit.

Gomes goes on to show that since the southern defenders of slavery treated the New Testament as a blueprint or a rulebook,

> they could have cited with equal approval Titus 2:9-10, "Bid slaves to be submissive to their masters and to give satisfaction in every respect; they are not to be refractory, nor to pilfer, but to show entire and true fidelity, so that in everything, they may adorn the doctrine of God our Saviour." And they could have added Paul's advice to the Ephesians, repeated also in Colossians, where he urges slaves to be obedient to their masters in the same way that they would obey Christ, "not in the way of eye service, as men-pleasers, but as servants of Christ, doing the will of God from the heart, rendering service with a good will as to the Lord and not men." (Ephesians 6:5-9)[7]

In constructing their case for slavery, white southerners also relied on the book of Philemon. There, Paul informs Philemon, a slaveowner, that he has converted his runaway slave, Onesimus. Rather than condemning the institution of slavery, Paul returns

---

6   Ibid., 90.

7   Ibid., 91.

Onesimus to his owner with the advice, "No longer treat him as a slave, but treat him as your brother." That was sufficient evidence for white slaveholders in the American South that God had sanctioned the institution of slavery.

On the other hand, when other Americans further north launched a wholesale attack on the institution of slavery, they also based their case on Scripture. But instead of arguing from prooftexts and rules drawn from a biblical blueprint, they argued from overarching biblical principles. They asked, for example, how slavery squares with what we know from Scripture about the nature of God and his kingdom. Thus, if God is love, and if we assume he extends his love to all people, how can we then hold slaves? Again, if Christ died for all human beings, how can we then hold slaves? We know that Scripture does not say, "God was in Christ, reconciling white men to himself." Instead, it clearly affirms that "God was in Christ reconciling the world to himself." How can we then hold slaves? Or again, if "in Jesus Christ there is neither slave nor free, Jew nor Greek, male nor female," how can we then hold slaves? This radically different way of understanding the Bible fueled the abolitionist movement that eventually brought the institution of slavery crashing to the ground.

The point is clear. There are two ways of reading the Bible. We can treat the Bible as a blueprint, a constitution, or a rulebook. Or we can treat the Bible as a narrative that tells the story of God's mighty deeds on behalf of the world which he created, which he seeks to redeem, and over which he someday will triumph when his rule is complete. The Baconian approach forces us to address social and ethical issues only from the standpoint of blueprints and prooftexts, while the narrative approach allows us to address those issues from the standpoint of fundamental biblical principles. While the Baconian, blueprint conception of the

Bible has dominated the history of our movement, many of our people, especially in the nineteenth century, also embraced an apocalyptic perspective that focused on the mighty acts of God and his final triumph over all the earth. Based on that perspective, they had a clear vision of what the Kingdom of God should look like in the here and now. And based on that vision, they were able to address social issues like poverty, slavery, racism, and war in fundamentally biblical ways.

Two Hermeneutic Approaches & the Question of Women in the Church

We have explored the question of slavery from the standpoint of a Baconian reading of the biblical text, on the one hand, and a narrative reading of the biblical text, on the other. Now we must ask how these two hermeneutic principles might work if we apply them to a contemporary issue, namely, the role of women in the church.

It is clear that if we think of the Bible as nothing more than a blueprint, then there is no question about the proper role of women in the church: they must be silent. Any number of passages make this clear. The two passages most often cited in this regard are 1 Corinthians 14:33-35 and 1 Timothy 2:11. 1 Corinthians 14:33-35 clearly states,

> As in all the congregations of the saints, women should remain silent in the churches. They are not allowed to speak, but must be in submission, as the Law says. If they want to inquire about something, they should ask their own husbands at home; for it is disgraceful for a woman to speak in the church.

The 1 Timothy passage reads as follows:

> A woman should learn in quietness and full submission. I do not permit a woman to teach or to have authority over a man; she must be silent. For Adam was formed first, then Eve.

But what if we addressed this question from the standpoint of God's mighty deeds? What does it mean to say that "God so loved the world that he gave his only begotten Son"? Should we understand that passage to mean that God so loved the *men of the world* that he gave his only begotten Son? What does it mean to say that "God was in Christ reconciling the world to Himself"? Should we understand that passage to mean that God was in Christ reconciling *only men* to himself? Or what does Paul mean when he writes in Galatians 3:26-9,

> You are all sons of God through faith in Christ Jesus, for all of you who were baptized into Christ have clothed yourselves with Christ. There is neither Jew nor Greek, slave nor free, male nor female, for you are all one in Christ Jesus. If you belong to Christ, then you are Abraham's seed, and heirs according to the promise.

It is clear that we will get two very different answers to this question depending on the hermeneutic principle we use to understand the biblical text.

The problem that we must then face is how to reconcile these two answers. What happens when New Testament rules—or, at least, what we think are New Testament rules—seem to clash with fundamental New Testament principles? Should the principles give way to the rules, or should the rules give way to the principles?

We can shed light on this question if we can return once again to the question of slavery. We would all agree that the New Testament principle in this regard is clear: slavery is inconsistent with the Kingdom of God, in spite of the fact that many New Testament passages seem to legitimate that institution. Slavery is inconsistent with the Kingdom of God because it is inconsistent with the person of God, and because it is inconsistent with the mighty deeds God has performed and will perform when he finally triumphs over all the earth.

Likewise, we could argue that subjugation of women, though seemingly legitimated by many isolated passages, is nonetheless inconsistent with the Kingdom of God because it is inconsistent with the person of God, and because it is inconsistent with the mighty deeds God has performed and will perform when he finally triumphs over all the earth. This is why Tim Woodroof perceptively commented,

> As Christians, we must begin with an understanding of the values and community ethic which are expected to shape God's new community. Are sexual distinctions so vital in the church that spirituality, giftedness, [and] maturity must forever bow before that one criterion? If both male and female are of equal value and worth to God, if both are saved in the same way, if both are added to the new community, and if, in this community, an ethic prevails where relationships are determined by mutual submission, ... then don't we come perilously close to importing ancient cultural norms into the church by reifying distinctions according to sex and insisting on role relationships that have more to do with societal values than with kingdom principles?[8]

Finally, if our task is to conform ourselves to kingdom principles, not to cultural values, how then can we explain the fact that Paul sent the slave Onesimus back to the slave owner Philemon and never once challenged the institution of slavery? Might it be reasonable to assume that Paul never attempted to dismantle the institution of slavery because he knew he couldn't? Slavery was thoroughly entrenched in the Roman Empire during New Testament times. Paul knew that when the Kingdom of God came in its fullness, "there would be neither slave nor free." But in the meantime, the best Paul could hope to do was to transform the slave/master relationship,

---

8 Tim Woodroof, lectureship presentation, Pepperdine University Lectureship, 1997.

and this is precisely what he sought to do in passage after passage in our New Testament.

How is this insight pertinent to the question regarding the role of women in the church? Just as we know a great deal about slavery in the Roman Empire, we also know a great deal about the role of women in the Empire. We know that in the context of the Empire, women had very little worth. They were to be seen, but not heard. Much the same was true in Jewish culture, a point that Paul acknowledges when he writes, "They are not allowed to speak, but must be in submission, as the Law says." Is it possible that when Paul denied women the right to speak in the churches, he simply sought to conform to the overpowering norms of Roman and Jewish culture in his day? At the same time, however, that same Paul offered an enduring biblical principle which transformed the male/female relationship in the body of Christ: "There is neither male nor female, for you are all one in Christ Jesus."

Conclusions

The question of the role of women in the church is one that troubles many congregations of Churches of Christ and one for which I surely do not have all the answers. But I do know that there is more than one way to read the Bible. And so I offer this analysis in the hopes that it might provide one more perspective on the biblical text as we seek to sort through this thorny problem.

As I conclude this chapter, I want to return to the issue with which we began—the seductive power of the culture in which we live. In that regard, I want to suggest that there are many ways in which we can find ourselves in bondage to culture. We can certainly be in bondage to our contemporary culture if we rush to empower women in the church only because women are now empowered in the larger culture. At the same time, we can find ourselves in bondage to an ancient culture if, in our effort to follow the commands, examples, and inferences of the biblical text, we seek to bind ourselves to practices of the ancient church that more closely reflect the norms of the ancient world than the norms of biblical faith. I submit that we will find the norms of biblical faith not by treating the Bible as a blueprint and reading it from an eighteenth-century scientific perspective, but by treating the Bible as a narrative that tells us the story of the mighty acts of God.

s e v e n

WHY RESTORATIONISTS DON'T FIT THE EVANGELICAL MOLD; WHY CHURCHES OF CHRIST INCREASINGLY DO[1]

For the most part, American Protestants on both sides of the aisle—evangelicals as well as mainline Protestants—have little or no comprehension of the meaning of the "restoration vision." Whether one employs the term "restorationism" or "primitivism," most find the very concept foreign if not incomprehensible, eccentric, and odd.

Yet, there have always existed in American religious life communities of faith that can only be described as restorationist. Though rooted in the Protestant Reformation, these people generally have denied that they were Protestants at all, claiming instead the more universal label of "Christian." And when American Protestantism fractured into modernism and fundamentalism as the twentieth century dawned, restorationists often refused to identify themselves with either camp. Instead, they were loyal to what they perceived as the most

---

1   This chapter first appeared in *Re-Forming the Center: American Protestantism, 1900 to the Present*, Douglas Jacobsen and William Vance Trollinger, Jr., eds., (Grand Rapids: Eerdmans, 1998). Used by permission of the publisher.

ancient forms of Christian faith and practice reflected in Christian scripture. From their perspective, liberals and evangelicals alike had courted the world's favor, and restorationists therefore judged them both as severely compromised versions of the Christian faith and, in many ways, mirror images of one another.

Mainline Protestants, Evangelicals & the "Restoration Vision"

What might we say of the mainline Protestant assessment of the restoration vision?

The noted Methodist churchman and historian, Albert Outler, typified that assessment when he chanced to witness, some years ago, on a church building in Sweetwater, Texas, a cornerstone that read,

> The Church of Christ
> Founded at Jerusalem
> AD 33
> Organized in Sweetwater
> AD 1882
> This Building Erected, 1907

Outler was dumbfounded. The following summer, he shared this story with friends at the Third World Conference of Faith and Order in Lund, Sweden, but the story drew only "quizzical smiles—and, occasionally, polite incredulity."

Over the next several years, Outler repeatedly told his wife about this curious stone, but she responded with utter disbelief. Finally, Outler determined to show her the evidence. The two of them made the 200-mile trek west from Dallas to Sweetwater, only to discover that the old building with the curious cornerstone was gone. A new building now stood several miles away, but the old cornerstone was nowhere to be found.

Increasingly desperate to show his wife the hard, tangible evidence for this implausible artifact, Outler located the minister and politely asked

him what had happened to the stone. A majority
in the church, the minister explained, did not wish
the old stone in the new building, and the stone
now rested in the yard of the local stone mason.
Delighted, Outler located the stone, photographed
it from every possible angle, then arranged for a flat
bed truck to haul the stone from Sweetwater to the
university museum at Texas Christian University in
Fort Worth, just in case, as Outler explained, "pos-
terity is ever interested."[2]

95

*Why
Restorationists
Don't Fit the
Evangelical
Mold; Why
Churches
of Christ
Increasingly Do*

Though this stone reflects a worldview that
characterizes all restorationist traditions to one
degree or another, Outler's response of disbelief
that such a stone—and such a perspective—could
exist typifies the fundamental failure of mainline
Protestants to comprehend what the restoration
vision is all about.

One might think that evangelicals understand
the restoration ideal better than do their counter-
parts in mainline Protestantism, but that plainly
is not the case. For many years, I indulged myself
in the supposition that modern evangelicals bear
a strong and special kinship to restorationists. I
imagined this was true since evangelicals share with
restorationists an intense allegiance to the Bible
as the one and only source of Christian truth, and
especially since so many evangelical historians have
claimed Churches of Christ, Mennonites, and other
restorationist traditions as part of the evangelical
alliance.[3]

Recently, however, I determined to rethink my
assumptions regarding the relation between evan-

---

2 Albert Outler, "Church History By the Cube," *Mission
   Journal* 20 (March 1987): 30-1.

3 Cf. George Marsden, Understanding *Fundamentalism and
   Evangelicalism* (Grand Rapids: Eerdmans, 1991), 5; James
   Davidson Hunter, "Operationalizing Evangelicalism: A
   Review, Critique & Proposal," *Sociological Analysis* 42
   (1981): 370.

gelicals and restorationists. I began that process by reflecting on the history of my own tradition, the Churches of Christ. Before we explore that relationship in the context of the Churches of Christ, a brief introduction to the history of that tradition is in order.

Born on the American frontier in the early nineteenth century, the Churches of Christ were originally part of a wide-ranging movement that sought to unify all Christians by appealing to the Bible alone and to the simplicity and the ethical power of the early Christian communities. In those early years, they answered to the label, "Churches of Christ," but also to the terms, "Disciples of Christ" and "Christian Churches."

In that founding period, they looked for leadership especially to two men: Barton W. Stone and Alexander Campbell. In many ways, Stone bore the earmarks of a genuine evangelical. A child of the revivals, he stood in debt to the Great Awakening in several ways and then, in 1801, played a key role in the Cane Ridge Revival that helped ignite the Second Great Awakening. He fraternized with the evangelical denominations and recognized their members as brothers and sisters in Christ. And yet, Stone was also profoundly restorationist, even countercultural in orientation. At the heart of his thought stood a New Testament ethic that he grounded in the biblical promise that the Kingdom of God would finally triumph over all the world. Stone took this promise very seriously, and believed this ethic could provide the foundation on which all Christians could unite.

Equally ecumenical but less focused on ethics than Stone, Alexander Campbell believed that unity could best be achieved through a progressive, rational reconstruction of the ancient Christian church, based on an almost scientific reading of the biblical text. For a variety of reasons, Campbell's influence slowly eclipsed that of Stone beginning in 1823.

Then, in 1832, the Stone and Campbell movements joined forces and soon became the largest indigenous Christian movement in the United States. By the late nineteenth century, however, this erstwhile ecumenical movement finally divided into two distinct denominations: Disciples of Christ and Churches of Christ. The Disciples carried Campbell's progressive and ecumenical spirit into the twentieth century and finally rejected the restoration vision altogether. At the same time, the Churches of Christ coalesced around the other side of the nineteenth-century platform: the restoration of the ancient Christian faith/church. For them, restoration embodied not only the rational reconstruction of the ancient Christian church—an emphasis they inherited from Campbell; restoration also entailed a countercultural commitment to biblical ethics—an emphasis they inherited from Barton W. Stone.[4]

This was the tradition in which I was raised and the tradition to which I turned my attention as I began to reflect on the possible relation between evangelicalism and the restorationist heritage.

I began my reflections by reminding myself that in my own lifetime, Churches of Christ have seldom fraternized with any of the organizations one normally associates with the evangelical world. They have never sustained a connection to the National Association of Evangelicals and, until recently, none of the dozen or so colleges related to Churches of Christ has ever

---

4   Several texts trace the history of this tradition. See, for example, Earl Irvin West's four-volume *Search for the Ancient Order* (vol. 1: Nashville: Gospel Advocate Co., 1964; vol. 2: Religious Book Service, 1950; vol. 3: Religious Book Service, 1979; and vol. 4: Religious Book Service, 1987); Robert Hooper's *A Distinct People: A History of the Churches of Christ in the Twentieth Century* (West Monroe, LA: Howard Publishing, 1993); Leroy Garrett's *The Stone-Campbell Movement: An Anecdotal History of Three Churches*, rev. ed. (Joplin, MO: College Press, 1994); and Richard Hughes's *Reviving the Ancient Faith: The Story of Churches of Christ in America* (Grand Rapids: Eerdmans, 1996).

belonged to the evangelically-oriented Council for Christian Colleges and Universities.[5] The truth is, for most of my lifetime, the formal ties that might have connected Churches of Christ to the evangelical world have been virtually nonexistent.

With that in mind, I began reading again George Marsden's book, *Understanding Fundamentalism and Evangelicalism.* I thought it would help if I compared the history of Churches of Christ to Marsden's description of evangelicals at every significant point.

Marsden observed first of all that evangelicals trace their American roots to the great revivals of Whitefield, Finney, Moody, Sunday, and Graham.[6] I realized that though I had grown up in Churches of Christ, a denomination Marsden labels "evangelical,"[7] I had never heard of Whitefield, Finney, Moody, or Sunday until I was in graduate school. Until then, I knew little or nothing about the evangelical revivalist tradition.

In that light, I was surprised to find that Marsden identifies Alexander Campbell, one of the nineteenth-century "fathers" of Churches of Christ, as "a revivalist."[8] The truth is, Campbell was not a revivalist in any sense. In fact, Campbell strenuously opposed most of the revivals of his age on the grounds that they substituted emotion for the plain word of God.

---

5   Abilene Christian University (Abilene, TX) was the first educational institution related to Churches of Christ to join the Council for Christian Colleges and Universities, having done so on July 26, 1995. As of this writing, three other institutions have followed in ACU's footsteps: Oklahoma Christian University, David Lipscomb University, and Ohio Valley College.

6   Marsden, *Understanding Fundamentalism and Evangelicalism,* 2.

7   Ibid., 5.

8   Ibid., 67.

If Campbell was a revivalist, one might rightly expect to find favorable references to Charles Finney in Campbell's *Millennial Harbinger* which he edited for virtually the duration of Finney's career. Yet, for over thirty years, only three references appear, and none of them were favorable. Two of the three, in fact, chided Finney on explicitly restorationist grounds: he had substituted "the anxious bench" for baptism and replaced the ancient gospel with his "new measures."[9]

Campbell, in fact, thought that revivals offered little more than "the machinery of 'getting religion' by animal excitement." He complained that

> the doctrine of American Revivals, so rife since the year 1734, has made Methodists of all the Protestants in America, except a few genteel Episcopalians, whose love of good breeding, more than their knowledge of the gospel, has prevented them from screaming, swooning, fainting, jerking, laughing, shouting, under "the influence of the Holy Ghost," as they express it.

Further, Campbell claimed that biblical illiteracy abounded especially among those caught up in the revivals. "I should not be believed," he wrote, "were I to tell half of what I know of the ignorance of the Book in this religious, enthusiastic, and fanatical population."[10]

Again, Marsden notes that three traditions that helped give shape to twentieth-century evangelicalism—dispensationalism, holiness, and pentecostalism—all revered Dwight Moody's lieutenant, Reuben Torrey.[11] What, then, of Churches of Christ? Did they revere Torrey as well? To answer that

9 Alexander Campbell, "Elder Finney's Substitute for Baptism," *Millennial Harbinger*, New Series, 5 (March 1841): 141; Discipulus, "Charles G. Finney," *Millennial Harbinger*, New Series, 5 (December 1841): 591-3.

10 Campbell, "Letter to Elder William Jones. No. VI," *Millennial Harbinger* 6 (August 1835): 355.

question, I searched the index to the most powerful paper circulated among Churches of Christ in those years, the *Gospel Advocate*, published in Nashville, Tennessee. Torrey's name never appears.

Or again, Marsden notes that "during the 1950s and 1960s the simplest...definition of an evangelical...was 'anyone who likes Billy Graham.'"[12] Yet, in my memory, Churches of Christ never much liked Billy Graham for essentially the same reasons Alexander Campbell never much liked Charles Finney. Indeed, the indexes to a variety of journals circulated among Churches of Christ for the past forty years reveal almost no references to Graham at all, and the few that did appear were largely negative.[13]

Most telling of all, Marsden observes that in the evangelical world, "denominational affiliation was ultimately a matter of free choice.... If you did not like one church, you could simply leave and go to the one down the street."[14] Nothing could be more foreign to the authentically restorationist mind, and certainly nothing could be more foreign to Churches of Christ, at least until recent years.

Restorationists & Evangelicals: The Fundamental Difference

There are many points at which one might compare restorationists—and especially Churches of Christ—with the broad evangelical tradition. One

---

11 Marsden, *Understanding Fundamentalism and Evangelicalism*, 43-4.

12 Ibid., 6.

13 Cf. Fred B. Walker, "Billy Graham in the Nation's Capitol," *Gospel Advocate* 94 (28 February 1952): 130-1; G. K. Wallace, "'My Answer,'" *Gospel Advocate* 117 (4 September 1975): 565-6.

14 Marsden, *Understanding Fundamentalism and Evangelicalism*, 17 and 81.

might explore worship styles, lifestyles, theology, or a host of other categories. In fact, in another essay, I have compared Churches of Christ with evangelicals from a theological perspective.[15] The present essay, however, focuses on ethics, politics, and culture since, in my view, the genius of the restoration vision finally has more to do with ethics than with theology.

Obviously, the comparisons I have already drawn are not definitive. Instead, they serve as clues to a deeper and wider gulf that separates restorationists from evangelicals. Navigation of that gulf requires a brief assessment of the cultural and political meaning of evangelicalism. We begin with John Calvin, clearly a sixteenth-century hero for most American evangelicals. Though a restorationist of sorts who liked to compare "the ancient church" with what he viewed as Catholic corruptions,[16] Calvin concerned himself chiefly with the sovereignty of God which he longed to impose over all the earth, beginning with Geneva.

Other Reformed leaders sounded the same refrain. Martin Bucer, for example, dedicated his *De Regno Christi* to Edward VI, King of England, in 1550. Also a restorationist of sorts, Bucer argued in that book that England could become the Kingdom of Christ only by restoring the faith and practice of the ancient church. Significantly, however, Bucer defined the ancient church in explicitly Constantinian terms. He described "the period of Constantine and the emperors who followed him" as a period in which "nothing [was] wanting ... in

---

15   Richard T. Hughes, "Are Restorationists Evangelicals?" in Donald Dayton and Robert K. Johnston, eds., *The Variety of American Evangelicalism* (Knoxville: University of Tennessee Press, 1991), 109–34.

16   Cf. John C. Olin, ed., *John Calvin/Jacopo Sadoleto: A Reformation Debate* (1966; Reprinted Grand Rapids: Baker Books, 1976).

regard to the happiness of the Church of Christ"
and a period "when churches were raised up all over
the world and flourished in exceptional piety."[17] In
this way, Calvin, Bucer, and virtually all Reformed
theologians perpetuated the old medieval vision of
Christendom, though now in Protestant guise.

Joel Carpenter cast further light on this issue
when he wrote that American fundamentalists also
were restorationists of sorts. They, too, valued both
scripture and the Christian past. But the past they
valued most was not the past of the first Christian
age, but rather "the past since the Protestant
Reformation."

> Fundamentalists assumed that primitive
> Christianity had already been restored at
> the Reformation and revived several times
> since then. Their task, then, was not to
> recover it, but to defend, cultivate, and pro-
> mote it....[18]

Carpenter should have added that the slice of the
Reformation that fundamentalists valued most
was the magisterial reform of Luther, Calvin, and
Zwingli.

This is the context in which we must understand the genius of American evangelicalism: most
evangelicals have sought "to defend, cultivate, and
promote" the heritage of the magisterial reformation, to Christianize the culture in which they live,
and to bring it under the sovereign sway of a distinctly Protestant God. There have been exceptions
to this pattern, to be sure. J. Gresham Machen, for
example, never fit this mold, as Darryl Hart points
out.[19] For the most part, however, evangelicals

---

17   Martin Bucer, "De Regno Christi" in Wilhelm Pauck, ed.,
     Melanchthon and Bucer, The Library of Christian Classics, vol.
     19, (Philadelphia: The Westminster Press, 1969), 209.

18   Joel Carpenter, "Contending for the Faith Once Delivered:
     Primitivist Impulses in American Fundamentalism" in
     Richard T. Hughes, ed., *The American Quest for the Primitive
     Church* (Urbana: University of Illinois Press, 1988), 101.

have never fully abandoned the old Constantinian model, even in the United States. Here one finds the meaning of the title Sidney Mead gave to one of his books: *The Old Religion in the Brave New World.*[20]

Inescapably, this was the cultural significance of virtually all the revivals to which evangelicals trace their identity. In this context, the Second Great Awakening is perhaps the most notable case in point. When evangelical Protestants realized the full implications of the First Amendment to the Constitution, they sought to create through persuasion what they no longer could achieve through coercion or force of law, namely a Protestant America. Further, since the nation's Founders sought to undermine all religious establishments, many evangelicals attacked those Founders as "infidels" whose alleged immorality would inevitably corrupt the nation. In this way, "a great tidal wave of revivalism" virtually drowned the "infidelity" that characterized the nation's founding, as Sidney Mead has pointed out time and again.[21]

Marsden confirms Mead's assessment of these events, but from a distinctly evangelical point of view. Given the nature of its founding, Marsden writes, one might expect that America might well "have adopted a genial democratic humanism, freed from explicitly Christian dogmas and institutions." However,

19   Darryl Hart, "J. Gresham Machen, Confessional Presbyterianism, and the History of Twentieth-Century Protestantism," chapter seven in Douglas Jacobsen and William Vance Trollinger, eds., *Reforming the Center: American Protestantism, 1900 to the Present* (Grand Rapids: Eerdmans, 1998).

20   Sidney E. Mead, *The Old Religion in the Brave New World: Reflections on the Relation between Christendom and the Republic* (Berkeley: University of California Press, 1977).

21   Sidney E. Mead, The *Lively Experiment* (New York: Harper and Row, 1963), p. 53; *The Nation with the Soul of a Church* (New York: Harper and Row, 1975), 122.

the fact that America had not in the nineteenth century followed the course set in the eighteenth by leaders like Franklin and Jefferson was due largely to vigorous evangelical enterprise. The United States had not drifted religiously during the nineteenth century. It had been guided, even driven, by resourceful evangelical leaders who effectively channeled the powers of revivals and voluntary religious organizations to counter the forces of purely secular change.[22]

Those revivals were so successful that Robert Baird, in his 1856 celebration of evangelical Protestantism in America, could describe the United States as "a Protestant empire" and "the most powerful of all Protestant kingdoms."[23] And Marsden concedes that by the time of the Gilded Age, "a Protestant version of the medieval ideal of 'Christendom' still prevailed."[24]

This is the context that illumines the cultural meaning of fundamentalism in the early twentieth century. If fundamentalists were evangelicals who were angry about something, as Jerry Falwell likes to suggest,[25] they were angry precisely because their longstanding domination of American culture was rapidly slipping away as the culture of modernism gained momentum.

This fact, in turn, sheds considerable light on the cultural meaning of the dispensational eschatology that most fundamentalists adopted in those years. Though there were exceptions, most evangelicals prior to the late nineteenth century had proclaimed a

---

22 Marsden, *Understanding Fundamentalism and Evangelicalism*, 11-12.

23 Robert Baird, *Religion in America, With Notices of the Unevangelical Denominations* (New York: Harper and Brothers, 1856), 32.

24 Marsden, *Understanding Fundamentalism and Evangelicalism*, 10.

25 Ibid., 1.

robust and highly optimistic *post*-millennial eschatology. America, they believed, was a Protestant empire whose goodness and righteousness would hasten the millennial dawn. Indeed, this conviction had prevailed among American evangelicals for at least one hundred and fifty years, from the Great Awakening to the close of the nineteenth century. One can only conclude that postmillennial optimism lay at the very heart of American evangelicalism through the close of the nineteenth century, and grew from their longstanding commitment to Constantinian assumptions and their own domination of American life and culture.

Then, suddenly, evangelicals made a radical about-face. They abandoned their optimistic, postmillennial faith and adopted instead its opposite: dispensational premillennialism. Why this sudden change? Clearly, the newfound premillennial theology was not central to historic evangelical thought. Rather it served as a weapon of last resort for fundamentalists who feared that modernism would erode and perhaps even destroy their evangelical empire.

Put another way, fundamentalists would fight modernism first with the weapon of biblical inerrancy. In case they lost that fight and therefore their control of the culture, they had another weapon close at hand. Jesus himself, they believed, would reimpose his control over American life in the coming millennial age, deal the modernists a stunning defeat, and rule with his evangelical saints for a thousand years. This simply means that postmillennialism and premillennialism were but two different ways of expressing the central concern of fundamentalists: the creation and maintenance of a Protestant civilization in the United States. One way or another, the fundamentalists finally would win.

If this portrayal of American evangelicalism is even remotely correct, then it contrasts dramatically with the historic concerns of restorationists.

At the most basic possible level, restorationists are Christians who yearn to return to the first Christian age. Some seek to recover the Pentecost experience of the Holy Ghost, as Grant Wacker, Edith Blumhofer, and Donald Dayton all have pointed out.[26] Others, like many Holiness denominations, seek to recover ancient norms for holy living. Still others, like Alexander Campbell, seek to reconstruct the forms and structures of the primitive church on a rational and scientific basis. Clearly, restorationists of all sorts are susceptible to illusions of innocence,[27] especially when they virtually identify themselves with one or another dimension of the first Christian age.

Yet, none of these concerns finally exposes the central core of the restorationist vision. That concern is simply this: the world is hopelessly corrupt, and by aligning itself with the world and its values, the church corrupted itself from an early date. There was, however, a golden age when the church had not yet fallen. The church must therefore embrace the values of that golden age when the world and the church had not yet formed their alliance. If this is the heart and soul of the restoration vision, it means that authentic restorationists are inevitably radical and countercultural

---

26 Cf. Edith L. Blumhofer, *Restoring the Faith: The Assemblies of God, Pentecostalism, and American Culture* (Urbana: University of Illinois Press, 1993), esp. 1–9; Grant Wacker, "Playing for Keeps: The Primitivist Impulse in Early Pentecostalism" in Hughes, ed., *The American Quest for the Primitive Church*, 196–219; Wacker, "Searching for Eden with a Satellite Dish: Primitivism, Pragmatism, and the Pentecostal Character" in Hughes, ed., *The Primitive Church in the Modern World* (Urbana: University of Illinois Press, 1995); and Donald W. Dayton, *Theological Roots of Pentecostalism* (Grand Rapids: Francis Asbury Press, 1987).

27 See, for example, Richard T. Hughes and C. Leonard Allen, *Illusions of Innocence: Protestant Primitivism in America, 1630–1875* (Chicago: University of Chicago Press, 1988).

Christians. This is why, in my judgment, the genius of the restoration vision is fundamentally ethical, not theological.

In this light, authentic restorationists would find themselves bewildered when Marsden explains how "remarkable" it was that "the specifically Christian aspects" of the American heritage did not erode more than they did under the withering "winds of frankly secular ideologies"[28] issuing from the deistic founders of the American nation. Authentic restorationists would find this concept difficult to comprehend, simply because the notions of a "Christian culture" or a "Christian America" make no sense in the context of the restorationist perspective.

For this reason, authentic restorationists of the early nineteenth century were typically not among those who maligned the founders for their alleged immorality and "infidelity." On the contrary, restorationists of that period generally praised the founders for doing what evangelicals had refused to do, that is, for rejecting all attempts to Christianize, much less to Protestantize, the United States. Those actions made it possible for restorationists to thrive in a way that they could not have thrived in a world controlled by evangelical Christians.

Thus, N. Summerbell, a spiritual descendant of New England's Elias Smith, criticized in 1847 those evangelicals who had "branded [Jefferson] with *Infidelity, Deism, and Atheism.*" To Summerbell, Jefferson's "religious views ... [were] as terrible to religious demagogues as were his political views to political tyrants." And when the followers of Barton Stone in Kentucky appealed to "the inalienable rights of free investigation [and] sober and diligent inquiry after [religious truth]," they implicitly praised the founders and condemned those evangelicals who still held out for

Why
Restorationists
Don't Fit the
Evangelical
Mold; Why
Churches
of Christ
Increasingly Do

28 Marsden, *Understanding Fundamentalism and Evangelicalism,* 11.

a Christian establishment in the United States.[29] This suggests that Nathan Hatch's *Democratization of American Christianity* chronicles not so much the thoughts and deeds of antebellum evangelicals as the thoughts and deeds of antebellum restorationists, though, unfortunately, Hatch never made that distinction.[30]

To put all this another way, the fundamental difference between evangelicals and restorationists is this: evangelicals subscribe to a model of Christian history that emphasizes continuity. Christian history, at least since the Reformation, is a seamless piece of cloth. This is why denominational loyalties have always been of small importance for most evangelicals. After all, evangelical Protestant churches of every stripe reflect the essence of the Reformation perspective. Further, to the extent that evangelicals seek to control the larger culture, they embrace a potential continuity between the church and the world, if only the world would submit to the sovereign rule of God.

On the other hand, the restorationist vision points to a radical tear in the fabric of Christian history. There is not the slightest possibility of continuity between the church and the world, and to the extent that Christians have made their peace with the world, the fabric of Christian history is badly torn.

Finally, however, we must acknowledge that evangelical theology and a restorationist understanding of what it means to live in the Kingdom of

---

29 N. Summerbell, "The Religious Views of Thomas Jefferson," cited in Alexander Campbell, "Christian Union—No. XI. Unitarianism," *Millennial Harbinger*, Series III, 4 (May 1847): 258–9; and J. and J. Gregg, "An Apology for Withdrawing from the Methodist Episcopal Church," *Christian Messenger*, 1 (December 25, 1826): 39–40.

30 Nathan O. Hatch, *The Democratization of American Christianity* (New Haven: Yale University Press, 1989).

God are not mutually exclusive perspectives. Surely there is no inherent tension between justification by grace through faith, for example, and Kingdom ethics. On the other hand, however, the restoration vision and Constantinian assumptions *are* mutually exclusive understandings.

Nonetheless, some evangelicals have employed an unmistakable appeal to the first Christian age, not as a tool for resistance and dissent but rather as the basis for creating a Christian political establishment. New England Puritans are perhaps the most notable case in point.[31] Yet, we must remember that when the restoration vision first emerged among England's earliest Puritans, it was nothing if not a tool for countercultural dissent. The Separatist Puritan tradition, eventually spawning Baptists, Quakers, and other radical dissenters who lived out of an unmistakably restorationist agenda, provides ample testimony to that dimension of the Puritan enterprise.

At the same time, living as they did when virtually everyone took for granted the notion of a Christian establishment, it was inevitable that some Puritans—most notably the Non-Separating Congregationalists of New England—would eventually employ the restoration vision as a tool for political power and domination. If there is a moral to this brief excursion, it is simply this: while a powerful dimension of nonconformity and dissent always lies at the heart of the restoration vision, restorationists can always employ that vision for precisely the opposite ends. When restorationists behave in this way, however, they have turned their backs on the genius of the vision they have claimed.

Scott Appleby reached similar conclusions in a paper that explored differences between restoration-

---

31 See Dwight Bozeman, *To Live Ancient Lives: the Primitivist Dimension of Puritanism* (Chapel Hill: University of North Carolina Press, 1988), who convincingly documents the restorationist theme in the New England Puritan experience.

ists and fundamentalists, especially in the context of Islam. Fundamentalists, Appleby argued, always seek political power in the larger culture. Though their rhetoric often appeals to the founding age, their chief concern is not to conform themselves to the norms of the founding age, but instead to control the modern world. "They are clearly involved," Appleby wrote, "in constructing a synthesis between" ancient norms and the modern world. Yet, the results of their efforts "demonstrate that … modernity is setting the terms for religious adaptation." For fundamentalists, therefore, appeals to the founding age are rhetorical, not substantive.

Restorationists, on the other hand, care little about political control over the modern world, but care deeply about individual and social moral transformation that takes its bearings from ancient norms. For this reason, Appleby described authentic restorationism as fundamentally prophetic. Restorationists, he argued, maintain a "prophetic stance toward the very kingdoms and nation-states that the fundamentalists seek to conquer." He therefore finally concluded, "The world … [restorationists] seek to restore does not sit easily with the ambition of modern world-conquerors," even when those conquerors are fundamentalists.[32]

Restoration Churches: Breeding Grounds for Evangelical Culture

The relation between the restoration and evangelical traditions in America, however, is more complex than I have suggested. The picture I have attempted to paint so far is a picture based on the beginnings of restoration traditions, when a vision of the primi-

---

32 R. Scott Appleby, "Primitivism as an Aspect of Global Fundamentalisms" in Hughes, ed., *The Primitive Church in the Modern World* (Urbana: University of Illinois Press, 1995), 31.

tive faith, undefiled by the world and its culture, still burns brightly. Such a picture would characterize not only the Churches of Christ, but Puritans, Pietists, Methodists,[33] Baptists, Latter-day Saints, Pentecostals, and a variety of holiness advocates in their earliest years. Though often evangelical in their theologies, all these movements began their careers with a distinctly restorationist orientation.

In America, however, the passion for the purity of first times, and the countercultural posture that passion has engendered, have always been difficult to retain. The allure of status and respectability in the larger culture has consistently eroded that commitment. When that commitment wanes, however, to whom can these churches go? To ask that question is to underscore the continued power of the two-party system of American Protestantism. There are really only two places restorationists might go: mainline Protestantism or evangelicalism.

Since the mainline for most of these people is not a serious option, restorationist churches constitute a perpetual feeder for the evangelical establishment. This is a way of saying that authentically restorationist churches are by definition sectarian. As they move toward denominational status, however, they almost invariably move into the orbit of evangelical Christianity. Restorationist churches, therefore, continually renew and refresh the evangelical establishment in America. This is one reason why historians of evangelicalism should take seriously the restorationist heritage in the United States.

Examples abound. American Mennonites began a flirtation with evangelicalism in the late nineteenth but especially in the early twentieth century when fundamentalist fervor was

---

33 Franklin H. Littell argues persuasively for the restorationist dimensions of early Methodism. Cf. Littell, "Assessing the Restoration Ideal" in Hughes, ed., *The Primitive Church in the Modern World*, 55-7.

at its height. That flirtation has not yet run its course, thanks chiefly to the Mennonites' historic emphasis on nonresistance.[34] On the other hand, Pentecostals in their earliest years were distinctly restorationist and radically countercultural, but moved quickly into the evangelical orbit, also during the heyday of fundamentalist hysteria. In part, this speedy transition doubtless resulted from the pragmatism that accompanied their primitivism, an unlikely pairing of qualities recently demonstrated by Grant Wacker.[35] One might also argue that Mennonites and Pentecostals alike were seduced by the illusion that fundamentalists were distinctly and inherently countercultural Christians like themselves, when in fact they were not, as we have seen.

There is, perhaps, no better example of the transition from restorationist sect to evangelical denomination than the Churches of Christ to whose story we must now return. There is no question that Campbell taught his followers the value of the restoration vision. Yet, like Calvin, Bucer, and other evangelicals before him, Campbell was only a "restorationist of sorts." After all, his restoration perspective had far more to do with a scientific reading of the biblical text than it did with the creation of countercultural Christian communities. Indeed, Campbell in many ways was an evangelical who, especially after 1837, sidled up to the evangelical establishment in his various efforts to promote a Protestant nation.[36]

---

34   James C. Juhnke, *Vision, Doctrine, War: Mennonite Identity
     and Organization in America, 1890–1930* (Scottdale,
     PA: Herald Press, 1989), 257–62; C. Norman Kraus,
     "Evangelicalism: A Mennonite Critique," in Dayton and
     Johnston, *The Variety of American Evangelicalism*, 193–4.

35   Wacker, "Searching for Eden with a Satellite Dish."

36   Cf. "From Primitive Church to Protestant Nation: The
     Millennial Odyssey of Alexander Campbell" in Hughes
     and Allen, *Illusions of Innocence*, 170–87.

On the other hand, Churches of Christ especially took their countercultural bearings from Barton W. Stone who combined his vision of primitive Christianity with a distinctly apocalyptic perspective.[37] For Stone, the Kingdom of God had expressed itself in the primitive church that was therefore normative for life, faith, and practice. But the Kingdom of God would come again soon in all its fullness. When that event transpired, God would rule over all the earth.

This perspective sounds remarkably like that of fundamentalists and evangelicals of the early twentieth century. Yet, there was a difference, for fundamentalists embraced an apocalyptic orientation only when they saw the evangelical domination of American life and culture in jeopardy. For them, affirming the expected triumph of the Kingdom of God was another way of saying that evangelical Christians would finally win the culture wars of the time, and that modernists inevitably would lose.

Stone, however, never sought to dominate the culture. Instead, he consistently rejected the values of the larger culture for the duration of his career. If fundamentalists finally threw their full weight behind a Christian America, Stone rejected the notion of a Christian America and even claimed that the Kingdom of God, when it manifested itself in its fullness, would finally subvert the United States along with all other political institutions.[38]

There are two notable measures of Stone's countercultural orientation. First, Stone freed his slaves in the aftermath of the revival, "choosing poverty in good conscience," as he put it, "to all the treasures of the world." Soon, other Kentucky

37 Apocalyptic in this context should not be confused with premillennial. On this point, see Hughes, *Reviving the Ancient Faith*, 3 and 92–3.

38 Barton W. Stone, "Reflections of Old Age," *Christian Messenger* 13 (August 1843): 123–6.

Christians loyal to Stone moved to Ohio where they also freed their slaves. These events transpired long before most southerners had seriously considered such a course of action.[39] Second, Stone shared with Mennonites an uncompromising commitment to the principles of pacifism and nonviolence. Stone saw clearly the radical tear in the fabric of history that all restorationists discern. He therefore turned his back on the culture of his age and cast his lot with the Kingdom of God, both as it was in the ancient church and as he expected it to be when the fullness of the Kingdom of God finally arrived.

David Lipscomb was the great third-generation leader of Churches of Christ whose influence dominated that tradition from the Civil War to the early twentieth century. Lipscomb reflected Stone's countercultural views almost perfectly. Though a man of some means, he identified with the outcast and the poor, resisted racial discrimination, and refused to vote or fight in wars. More important, Lipscomb grounded his countercultural behavior squarely in his apocalyptic orientation that prompted him to confidently expect the final triumph of the Kingdom of God and "the complete and final destruction ... of the last vestige of human governments and institutions."[40] More important still, Lipscomb thought these convictions reflected the very "key notes ... of the Old and New Testaments." Without them, he said, the Bible was "without point or meaning."[41]

In that light, it is hardly surprising that when the *Ecclesiastical Almanac* placed Churches of Christ in

39 Barton W. Stone, *The Biography of Eld. Barton W. Stone* (Cincinnati, 1847), 44; Joseph Thomas, *The Travels and Gospel Labors of Joseph Thomas* (Winchester, VA, 1812), 56.

40 David Lipscomb, *Civil Government* (Nashville, 1889), 25 and 27-8.

41 Lipscomb, *Civil Government*, 25, 27-8 (cf. 83-4), 96.

the evangelical orbit, Lipscomb called the *Almanac*'s report both "false and slanderous."[42]

There can be no doubt that Lipscomb's radical posture declined in popularity among Churches of Christ as the nineteenth century wore on. After all, many took their bearings more from Campbell than they did from Stone. These "Campbellites" defined the restoration vision more as a scientific recreation of the forms and structures of ancient Christianity than as a recreation of countercultural communities identified with the Kingdom of God. Yet, Lipscomb's vision persisted with remarkable strength, especially in Middle Tennessee and the surrounding regions.

Then, between 1915 and 1960, Churches of Christ fought two great intramural wars. When those wars were over, Churches of Christ essentially had abandoned their posture as a restorationist sect and emerged more and more as an evangelical denomination. The first of those wars centered on premillennial eschatology, a battle that mainly served to symbolize a much deeper issue: the validity of the apocalyptic perspective, inherited from Stone and Lipscomb.

To understand this struggle, we must first realize that, in the late nineteenth century, Churches of Christ suffered a disastrous division from the Disciples of Christ. In almost every city, the Disciples took the bulk of the members and the bulk of the wealth. Now relegated to the "wrong side of the tracks," Churches of Christ were left virtually to begin again, especially in urban areas.

World War I erupted in 1914, and found Churches of Christ seeking to compensate for their diminished standing. Specifically, they sought numerical growth and respectability. But it would be exceedingly difficult for Churches of Christ to

---

42 Lipscomb, "The Question Settled," *Gospel Advocate* 11 (March 11, 1869): 224.

gain many members or much respect in the crusading climate of World War I. After all, many of their members had committed themselves both to pacifism and to an apocalyptic outlook that judged the nation and found it wanting. Not surprisingly, leaders of Churches of Christ now took steps to scuttle the apocalyptic worldview.

This issue played itself out over dispensational premillennialism, a viewpoint that a small minority among Churches of Christ had embraced. The mainstream of Churches of Christ, however, rejected the premillennial vision and literally purged the church of its premillennial sympathizers. By the time they had finished their work, the entire apocalyptic vision among Churches of Christ—including the pacifist tradition—was essentially dead. Predictably, by the 1930s, significant segments of Churches of Christ joined the Protestant crusade for old-fashioned Americanism, anti-Communism, and the maintenance of a Christian America.

The destruction of the apocalyptic vision severely weakened both the restoration vision and the countercultural dimensions of Churches of Christ who increasingly made their peace with the spirit of the age. This became especially apparent in the aftermath of World War II, when the mainstream of Churches of Christ increasingly abandoned its nineteenth-century moorings in the interest of modernization, and sought to enter the mainstream of American culture as a "respectable denomination."

They did this through attempts to enhance their colleges by appealing to the budgets of local congregations, through a variety of promotional strategies, through increasingly complex institutional structures, and through a vast building campaign, aimed at giving Churches of Christ more visibility in the affluent and "respectable" parts of town. Many who maintained their allegiance to the values of nineteenth-century Churches of Christ saw these developments as nothing less than betrayal of the restoration vision. A bitter fight ensued, but when the dust finally settled in the late 1950s, the mainstream of Churches of Christ had essentially purged from their ranks those they labeled as "anti"—shorthand for the "anti-institutional" Churches of Christ.

117

*Why
Restorationists
Don't Fit the
Evangelical
Mold; Why
Churches
of Christ
Increasingly Do*

Following the 1960s, other developments suggested that Churches of Christ were rapidly turning their backs on their restorationist heritage and moving into the evangelical orbit. First, the legalism and exclusivism that had characterized many congregations for so long now gave way to the distinctly evangelical theme of justification by grace through faith. At the same time, a therapeutic gospel, coupled with an emphasis on "family values," both popular among evangelical churches in the aftermath of the 1960s, increasingly dominated many Church of Christ pulpits.[43] Worship sometimes verged on entertainment, and many urban congregations adopted "church growth" strategies that had more in common with the Willow Creek Church in Chicago than with the traditional restoration heritage. In these ways, Churches of Christ were completing a journey they had begun in the early twentieth century—a journey from restorationist sect to evangelical denomination.

Conclusions

So finally we return to the church in Sweetwater, Texas, and to the cornerstone that so amazed Albert Outler. But we must recall that Outler also took note of the fact that a majority in that congrega-

---

43   For an assessment of the therapeutic gospel in contemporary Protestantism, see Marsha G. Witten, *All Is Forgiven: The Secular Message in American Protestantism* (Princeton: Princeton University Press, 1993).

tion wanted a new building without the old stone. To Outler, this was nothing less than "rejection of a tradition of rejecting 'tradition.'"[44] But it was more than that. It also symbolized the fact that this congregation—along with Churches of Christ at large—was slowly turning its back on its restoration heritage. While the cornerstone took its place in a museum in Fort Worth, Texas, many Churches of Christ were taking their place in the American evangelical mosaic.

---

44   Outler, "Church History by the Cube," 31.

CONCLUSION

e i g h t

RECLAIMING A HERITAGE

It is by now a commonplace that Churches of Christ are suffering a severe identity crisis. This crisis has much to do with the time-honored restoration vision that was central to the agenda of Churches of Christ until very recent years. For a very long time, that vision was thoroughly linked to polity concerns, patternism, legalism, and even exclusivism. The questions we brought to the restoration vision were questions of form and method. What is the proper form of church organization? What are the proper forms for worship? What is the proper form of baptism? For celebrating the Lord's supper? For singing? Even now, at the beginning of the 21st century, many in our churches still think of the Christian faith in those terms that, for them, constitute genuine restorationism.

On the other hand, it is time to admit that in our churches, a wide variety of people from all walks of life—homemakers, businesspeople, lawyers, doctors, teachers, and day laborer—simply do not find patternism and legalism to be meaningful themes. Nonetheless, we have associated those themes with the restoration vision for so long that we hardly know how to conceptualize that vision in any other way. And so we throw the proverbial baby out with the bathwater. For many in our churches today, the restoration vision is a dead-end street, an essentially useless category.

121

And so we are left with no useful past, no clear identity, and no meaningful legacy. Essentially, we are spiritual orphans. We are left, therefore, to start again, to rethink the Christian faith from scratch. In a sense, rethinking the faith from scratch is consistent with the restoration vision. The problem is that we have largely abandoned the vision that would sustain us in that effort. Inevitably, therefore, we rethink the faith in someone else's terms, as if we have no meaningful story to tell. And that is the crux of the identity crisis that engulfs Churches of Christ today.

I am fully aware of the illusions the restoration vision can foster.[1] Nonetheless, we need to ask, is there another way to understand the restoration vision, a way that might redeem that vision for this generation but that, at the same time, would connect in meaningful and powerful ways with the history and heritage of Churches of Christ? To answer that question, I want to explore some neglected aspects of our own history.

The Anabaptist/Mennonite Heritage

Before I do that, however, I want to turn to another tradition that was profoundly restorationist, yet that defined the restoration vision in ways radically different from its definition in our fellowship, at least in the twentieth century. That tradition is sixteenth-century Anabaptism and its modern heir, the Mennonites.

In his pioneering book, *The Anabaptist View of the Church*, Franklin Littell explained that Anabaptism was fundamentally a restorationist movement.[2] Anabaptists, however, seldom spoke of polity issues. They seldom asked about form and

---

1 See Richard T. Hughes and C. Leonard Allen, *Illusions of Innocence: Protestant Primitivism in America, 1630–1875* (Chicago: University of Chicago Press, 1988).

2 Franklin H. Littell, *The Anabaptist View of the Church: A Study in the Origins of Sectarian Protestantism* (2d ed.; Boston: Starr King, 1958).

method. Instead, they focused the restoration lens squarely on questions of lifestyle—what contemporary Mennonites refer to as radical discipleship.[2] For almost five hundred years, Mennonites have concluded that radical discipleship is a countercultural commitment. They have refused to fight, they have nurtured humility, they have served the poor and the dispossessed, and they have abandoned themselves for the sake of others. They have done all this for one reason: they sought to conform themselves to the pattern of the cross and to the teachings and examples of Jesus.

A case in point is the story of the Dutch Anabaptist, Dirk Willems. In 1569 the court issued a warrant for Willems' arrest, but when the sheriff and his deputy came to seize him, Willems had fled. According to the great Anabaptist chronicle, the *Martyr's Mirror*, it was the dead of winter, and Willems ran quickly across the frozen river, only to hear the deputy fall through the ice behind him. Willems knew full well that the deputy could not escape the water's icy grip alone. But he also knew that, if he returned to aid the deputy, he himself would be apprehended and likely killed. Willems, however, turned back and pulled the man to safety. When the sheriff arrived only minutes later, the deputy argued strongly that Willems should be spared. But the sheriff commanded that he be seized. Only days later, he was burned at the stake. This was the meaning of the restoration vision for sixteenth-century Anabaptists.[4]

---

3 Harold S. Bender defined this "Anabaptist vision" in his presidential address to the American Society of Church History in 1943. Enormously influential in Mennonite circles, that address helped shape the way many contemporary Mennonites understand their forebears and themselves. Bender elaborated on that vision in *The Recovery of the Anabaptist Vision* (Scottdale, PA: Herald Press, 1957).

4 Thieleman J. van Braght, comp., *The Bloody Theater or Martyrs Mirror* (Scottdale, PA: Herald Press, 1997), 741-3.

To this day, the restoration vision plays a meaningful role in the belief structure of many Mennonites, the heirs of the Anabaptists. For example, a few years ago, a young coed at Notre Dame asked one of her teachers, Gerald Schlabach, about his faith. Schlabach, a Mennonite and at that time a graduate teaching assistant, replied,

> Deep in our community ... lies an instinct to ... return to basic New Testament Christianity. I am not so sure as some Mennonites that this is ever possible, but if I have to choose, I'll certainly prefer the attempt to approximate New Testament Christianity over any later version.[5]

And what might this vision mean to Mennonites today? John Roth, a young history professor at Goshen College, insists that "radical discipleship" lies at the heart of that vision.

> Radical discipleship should continue to name the principalities and powers of the world, to denounce the political and economic injustices of our society, but it should also include many small and more humble acts of cultural defiance and transformation. [It might] mean staying married to one person for life. It might mean a sacrificial and personal commitment to children and the elderly—the most vulnerable in our society—putting their interests above our rights, even if it is inconvenient.... It might mean foregoing the quickest routes to vocational success by setting aside a portion of life for focused service.... None of these ... [are] great, heroic deeds of self-renunciation, but ... [rather,] natural expression[s] of the living presence of God woven into the very fabric of our daily lives.[6]

---

5   Letter from Gerald Schlabach to a student, University of Notre Dame, Fall 1994.

6   John D. Roth, "Living Between the Times: The Anabaptist Vision and Mennonite Reality Revisited," unpublished paper delivered at "Whither the Anabaptist Vision" conference, Elizabethtown College, June 1994.

Against this backdrop of the Anabaptist/ Mennonite understanding of the restoration vision, one can begin to understand why a variety of contemporary Mennonite scholars have severely criticized the restoration vision of the Churches of Christ. The late John Howard Yoder, for example, wrote years ago that our "narrowing of the restitution focus to formal polity issues may have contributed to discrediting the idea of restitution."[7]

As Franklin Littell explains, however, the problem was larger than that. Though formally a Methodist, Littell is Anabaptist to the core. We should not be surprised, therefore, to hear his claim that Churches of Christ embraced the rhetoric of restorationism, but seldom embraced its substance. In Littell's reading of our history, which was largely confined to his reading of Alexander Campbell, there was little sense of separation from the world, little or no engagement with countercultural Christianity, and little appreciation for any sort of radical Christian lifestyle. Instead, under Campbell's leadership, our movement conformed itself to the pattern of our culture, not to the pattern of the cross. Indeed, Littell argues, many in our movement confused the glories of the ancient church with the glories of the nation. "The sometime millennial goal," he wrote, "of a separated pilgrim people passing through to another age and another City was overpowered by the manifest blessings and vital appeal of America." But for Littell, there was even more. He writes:

> As an outgrouper, it seems to me that the bone that stuck in the throat, methodologically, was the insistence that the religious program qualify by the norms set by Scottish

7 John Howard Yoder, "Anabaptism in History" in Hans-Jurgen Goertz, ed., *Umstrittenes Taufertum, 1525-1975: Neue Forschungen* (Göttingen: Vandenhoeck & Ruprecht, 1975), 255.

Common Sense philosophy. The secure ground of a powerful myth or root metaphor was left behind, and vigorous minds entered into the intellectual controversies of the age as modernity defined them. To "stick to the facts," to proclaim Bible "facts," to authenticate religious truth by grafting it onto "the scientific method"—these are rules more readily related to vital civic life in nineteenth-century America than they are to what could be known and reclaimed from the life of early Christians at Corinth and Antioch and Ephesus. The stance of primitivism, which looks backward for its norms, was replaced by the spirit of modernity, looking blithely toward a future of progressive and orderly change.[8]

If Littell is correct, the identity crisis that Churches of Christ experience today is nothing new. Instead, it was built into the movement from its outset. The crisis lay in the fact that we employed the language of restoration and, by implication, of countercultural Christianity, but failed to actualize that vision. Instead, we settled for second best. We spoke of forms and methods instead of discipleship. We looked for "Bible facts" instead of models for holy living. And we focused on the Acts of the Apostles instead of on Jesus, the cross, and the Sermon on the Mount. And in the context of the book of Acts, we focused on Acts as facts instead of Acts as story. It was inevitable that, in time, the rhetoric of restoration would ring hollow in our ears.

This is not to suggest that all forms and structures are irrelevant or unimportant. To the contrary, some forms and structures are important to the extent that they symbolize the gospel message in powerful ways. For example, baptism by immersion is fundamental, not only because it symbolizes

---

8 Franklin Littell, "The Power of the Restoration Vision and Its Decline in Modern America," in Richard T. Hughes, ed., *The Primitive Church in the Modern World* (Urbana: University of Illinois Press, 1995), 61.

the death, burial, and resurrection of Christ, but also because it symbolizes a "new birth" for the believer. In this way, baptism points unwaveringly to the Kingdom of God which Jesus brought into the world, which he makes alive in us today, and which he will extend over all the earth when his rule is complete. But it is difficult to see much connection between the Kingdom of God and many of the concerns that we have placed on the center of the Christian stage.

The Other Side of the Story: The Early History of Churches of Christ

Yet there is another side to the story of Churches of Christ, a side that is little known and seldom told. This is the story that centers on Barton W. Stone, who taught Churches of Christ an entirely different understanding of the restoration vision. Stone concerned himself not so much with the forms and structures of the early church as with what it meant to live out one's life as a disciple in the Kingdom of God. And like the Mennonites, Stone understood discipleship in radical, countercultural ways. He therefore abandoned his ambitions for a lucrative legal career and gave his life to preaching—a commitment that brought him hardship and poverty for the rest of his days.

But there are other notable measures of Stone's countercultural orientation. First, Joseph Thomas tells us that the Kentucky Christians who followed Stone freed their slaves long before such a course was popular or even acceptable in the South. "I will observe that the Christians of these parts," Thomas wrote, "*abhor* the idea of *slavery*, and some of them have almost tho't that they who hold to slavery cannot be a Christian."[9] Further, Stone shared with

---

9 Joseph Thomas, *The Travels and Gospel Labors of Joseph Thomas* (Winchester, VA: n.p., 1812), 56.

Mennonites an uncompromising commitment to pacifism and nonviolence.

Stone's restoration vision, however, was not simply an appeal to the first Christian age. Instead, it was profoundly shaped by his apocalyptic orientation. In Timothy Weber's memorable phrase, Stone lived "in the shadow of the second coming."[10] This meant that for Stone, the final rule of God was not remote and far away. Instead, it was present in the here and now. He therefore sought to live his life as if the final triumph of the kingdom of God were a reality in this present world. This perspective lent Stone's faith a profoundly countercultural dimension.

There is no better illustration of Stone's apocalyptic, countercultural perspective than his position on politics. His premise was simply this:

> The lawful King, Jesus Christ, will shortly put them [human governments] all down, and reign with his Saints on earth a thousand years, without a rival.... Then shall all man made laws and governments be burnt up forever. These are the seat of the beast....

Following that premise, his conclusion was clear: "We must cease to support any other government on earth by our counsels, co-operation, and choice."[11] And so he refused even to vote, preferring instead to live his life under the singular rule of the Kingdom of God.

It is not my intention to hold up Stone's political orientation as a model for us today. Nor do I commend Stone's tendency to separate himself from the world's affairs. The Christian faith does not call us to isolate ourselves from the world, but to serve the world as salt, leaven, and light.

---

10 Timothy Weber, *The Living in the Shadow of the Second Coming: American Premillennialism, 1875-1925* (New York: Oxford University Press, 1979).

11 Barton W. Stone, "Reflections of Old Age," *Christian Messenger* 13 (August 1843): 123-6.

Nonetheless, there is much that we can learn from Barton W. Stone. In particular, I want to suggest that an apocalyptic orientation is vital to any serious restorationist perspective. Cut off from apocalyptic underpinnings, restorationism grows flat, wooden, and legalistic. Cut off from an apocalyptic orientation, we can imagine that God cares more about forms and structures and arbitrary rules than he does about how we treat other people in the name of Jesus Christ. And apart from apocalyptic understandings, our reading of the New Testament is inevitably colored more by the concerns of the culture in which we live than it is by God's own rule and kingdom.

Put in positive terms, an apocalyptic vision allows us to view both Scripture and the world from the perspective of God's final rule over all the earth. For that reason, an apocalyptic vision allows us to refocus our restorationist lens and prompts us to discover what is finally central in the biblical text. It therefore forces us to understand all of Scripture from the perspective of passages like this.

> When the Son of Man comes in his glory, and all the angels with him, he will sit on his throne in heavenly glory.... Then the King will say to those on his right, "Come, you who are blessed by my Father; take your inheritance, the kingdom prepared for you since the creation of the world. For I was hungry and you gave me something to eat, I was thirsty and you gave me something to drink, I was a stranger and you invited me in, I needed clothes and you clothed me, I was sick and you looked after me, I was in prison and you came to visit me." (Matt. 25:31-6)

Further, when we view the biblical text through an apocalyptic lens, we quickly discover that the great themes that define the final triumph of the Kingdom of God are the very same themes that defined the kingdom Jesus established two thousand years ago. Thus, when John's disciples asked Jesus if he was "the one who was to come, or should we expect someone else," Jesus replied,

Go back and report to John what you hear and see: The blind receive sight, the lame walk, those who have leprosy are cured, the deaf hear, the dead are raised, and the good news is preached to the poor. (Matt. 11:2-5)

Or again, when Jesus entered the synagogue in his home town of Nazareth, he took up the scroll and read from the book of Isaiah,

The Spirit of the Lord is on me,
  because he has anointed me
  to preach good news to the poor.
He has sent me to proclaim freedom for
  the prisoners
  and recovery of sight for the blind.
To release the oppressed,
  to proclaim the year of the Lord's favor....

Then Jesus explained, "Today this scripture is fulfilled in your hearing." (Luke 4:18-21)

Clearly, the Kingdom of God appeared in the life and work of the Son of God and will appear again in all its fullness in the final age. This means that the restoration vision and the apocalyptic vision are really two sides of the same coin and point to the same reality, the Kingdom of God. One who lives life in "the shadow of the Second Coming," therefore, lives life in the shadow of the first as well. For these reasons, a genuine restorationist is not one who, having settled comfortably into the present world, then seeks to recover the forms and structures of an ancient church. Rather, a genuine restorationist is one who embraces the values of the Kingdom of God. These are lessons we can learn from the restorationist and apocalyptic teachings of Barton W. Stone.

Later History of Churches of Christ

Stone's vision exerted an enormous impact on many in Churches of Christ throughout the nineteenth century. David Lipscomb, the great third-generation leader of our movement, especially embraced this perspective. Lipscomb refused to identify the

Church with the Kingdom of God. Instead, the Kingdom of God was the rule of God that would fill the earth in the last days, and he gave to that kingdom his unbending allegiance. For this reason, although a man of some means, he identified with the outcast and the poor, resisted racial discrimination, refused to vote or fight in wars, and worked tirelessly to relieve suffering and hurt in his own city of Nashville.

Yet by the waning years of the nineteenth century, fewer and fewer members of Churches of Christ related to Lipscomb's apocalyptic orientation or subscribed to his radical understanding of the Christian faith. Then, as the previous chapter explains—and as *Reviving the Ancient Faith* explains in even greater detail—Churches of Christ in the twentieth century fought two internal wars that essentially demolished the apocalyptic worldview that had been so important to this fellowship for so many years.

By the 1950s, in the aftermath of those wars, Churches of Christ were shell-shocked and battle-scarred. Our most immediate legacy was one of legalism, infighting, and ruptured congregations. We could hardly have been more poorly prepared to deal with the great moral and ethical issues that convulsed the nation in the 1960s. As a result, our churches, for the most part, either ignored those issues, thinking them irrelevant to the gospel message; or they implicitly—and sometimes explicitly—supported the racist and militarist structures that sparked the debates of those years. Not surprisingly, many of our brightest young people left Churches of Christ in that period. It is some comfort, at least, to realize that Stone, Lipscomb, and thousands of others who affirmed an apocalyptic/restorationist perspective in the nineteenth century would have addressed those same issues in very different ways. We know this because we know something of their record on similar kinds of concerns.

Since those years, Churches of Christ have sought to rebuild and recover some sort of meaningful identity. We have done this by focusing on the one theme that matters most in the Christian faith—the cross of Christ—and growing out of that theme, a newfound theology of grace. But we have not even begun to integrate our traditional restoration vision into this newly discovered biblical theology. The fact is that in many instances we could not integrate the two if we tried, and thus, to the extent that the restoration vision survives in our churches, our theology proceeds on two tracks that seem to have very little to do with each other.

We are faced, therefore, with several options. One is to abandon the restoration vision altogether. In my view, this option is singularly unhelpful since it cuts us off from our historic roots as a movement. It is rather like a divorce: it terminates the story that we, as a people, have been telling by virtue of our life together for a very long time.

The other option is to rethink and reaffirm our restoration heritage in ways more in keeping with the biblical witness—and more in keeping with our own particular history. But this would mean a radical shift for most of us in Churches of Christ. To affirm the restoration vision from a distinctly apocalyptic perspective, and to learn what it means to live life "between the times" would require us, in turn, to affirm ourselves as a radical, cross-centered, and countercultural people: At the very least, we must find some way to connect our history—the story of our life together—to the cross, not just to facts and forms, methods and structures.

There are two obstacles, however, that may block our path. In the first place, it may be that we are far too much at home with the world even to contemplate such a shift. In that light, the easiest path by far would be to continue our focus on forms, structures, and method. In the second place, we never have taken our own history seriously. Now, in more recent years, we may have so thoroughly abandoned the story of our common life together, along with its restoration vision, that we are beyond the point of return.

If either of these is true, then the handwriting is on the wall: the identity crisis that has plagued this movement for so long will not abate, but will only intensify until, finally, we tell a story that is not our own and our movement is virtually swallowed by one strain or another of the popular religious culture that dominates much of American Christianity today. That may be what a majority in Churches of Christ now want, but, if not, it is time to recognize the seriousness of the crisis that faces us and to begin to ask what we can do to address it.

ACU Press · ACU Box 29138 · Abilene, TX 79699 · fax: (915) 674-6471

American Origins *of* Churches *of* Christ

Three Essays on Restoration History

ISBN 0-89112-009-2
Trade paper, 118 pages
$19.95

Without question, the essays in this volume are landmarks in the historiography and self-understanding of the Stone-Campbell Movement, especially Churches of Christ. Written by two insiders and one outsider, each reflects significant developments in Stone-Campbell studies in the last forty years.... Read, learn, and enjoy!

—*from the Introduction by Douglas A. Foster*

ᕦᕤ

Richard Hughes is Distinguished Professor of Religion at Pepperdine University.

Nathan O. Hatch serves as Provost at Notre Dame University.

David Edwin Harrell, Jr. is the Breeden Eminent Scholar in the Humanities at Auburn University.

Douglas A. Foster is Associate Professor of Church History and Director of the Center for Restoration Studies at Abilene Christian University.

ᕦᕤ

Order from your favorite bookstore or call (800) 444-4228
Visit our website: www.acu.edu/acupress

Every congregation among us should have its adult classes use this succinct presentation of the history of Churches of Christ. Foster and Holloway have correctly presented material that demonstrates we have been a uniting, not a dividing, people.... *Renewing God's People* will become the standard text for passing down our history to the next generations.

—*Thomas H. Olbricht, Church Historian,*
author of Hearing God's Voice: My Life with Scripture in Churches of Christ

ε∞

Gary Holloway is Professor of Bible at Lipscomb University.

Douglas A. Foster is Associate Professor of Church History and Director of the Center for Restoration Studies at Abilene Christian University.

ε∞

Order from your favorite bookstore or call (800) 444-4228

Visit our website: www.acu.edu/acupress

A·C·U
PRESS

Renewing God's People
A Concise History of Churches of Christ

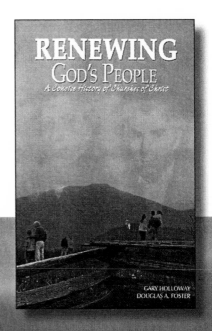

ISBN 0-89112-010-6
Trade paper, 151 pages
$14.95

ACU Press · ACU Box 29138 · Abilene, TX 79699 · fax: (915) 674-6471